Hey Rover, what's y

IF YOUR DOG is extremely r
sensitive stomach, she cou
easily bored and always eager to go for a ride,
you're probably sharing your home with a
Sagittarius.

This fun and engaging guide to your pet's inner
personality will help you understand why your one
cat has a constant need to coo and cuddle (must be
a Cancer!), while the other is happy to roam the
neighborhood all day in search of adventure and an
occasional fight (an Aries, no doubt).

Whether you worship the ground Rover walks
on—or curse the day you brought him home—
learning about his wacky, unpredictable ways
through his horoscope can help to strengthen the
bond you now share. The perfect gift for anyone
who shares his life with a creature great or small.

About the Author

Diana Nilsen (California) began her astrological studies in 1972. She hosted a metaphysical radio show in Los Angeles from 1995 to 1996 and teaches astrology and numerology in her home as well as at Los Angeles City College, where she is a full-time faculty member of Spanish and English.

To Write to the Author

If you wish to contact the author or would like more information about this book, please write to:

Diana Nilsen
℅ Llewellyn Worldwide
P.O. Box 64383, Dept. K488-X
St. Paul, MN 55164-0383, U.S.A.

Please enclose a self-addressed stamped envelope for reply, or $1.00 to cover costs. If outside U.S.A., enclose international postal reply coupon.

Your Pet's Horoscope

HOLD BOTH HANDLES

Diana
Nilsen

1998
Llewellyn Publications
St. Paul, Minnesota 55164 USA

FIRST EDITION
First Printing, 1998

Cover design: Lynne Menturweck
Cover and interior illustrations: Carrie Westfall
Book design and editing: Michael Maupin

Library of Congress Cataloging-in-Publication Data
Nilsen, Diana, 1953 –
    Your pet's horoscope / Diana Nilsen. -- 1st ed.
        p.   cm.
    ISBN   1-56718-488-X (pbk.)
    1. Astrology and pets.   I. Title.
BF1728.3.N55   1998
133.5'86360887--dc21   98-11167
                                                   CIP

Publisher's Note: Llewellyn Worldwide does not participate in, endorse, or have any authority or responsibility concerning private business transactions between our authors and the public.
    All mail addressed to the author is forwarded but, unless specifically instructed by the author, the publisher cannot give out an address or phone number.

Llewellyn Publications
A Division of Llewellyn Worldwide, Ltd.
P.O. Box 64383, Dept. K488-X
St. Paul, MN 55164-0383, U.S.A.

Printed in the United States of America.

This book is dedicated, in loving memory, to

Henry

A little brown Pisces bunny
who was a most treasured member of my family.

Contents

Introduction

SO YOU THOUGHT astrology was only for people? Wrong! The planetary influences that work through human beings actually affect all living things on Earth. There is a strong "connectedness" between the earth and all her children and the rest of our solar system. Webster's dictionary defines a "system" as being "a group of interacting bodies" (like planets) "under the influence of related forces." So, if humans are under the influence of these "forces," and we're all related in this system, the animals, too, are affected by this same influence. If they weren't, it would be illogical and not in keeping with the way the "system" works.

Animals don't have as complex a psychological make-up as humans, but they still have one. Animals also have feelings. The more developed the animal (like dogs, cats and some birds), the more these feelings are outwardly expressed. Even "less" developed animals (like rabbits, iguanas and ferrets) express some form of psychological and emotional well-being or lack thereof, and they don't all do it in the same way. Each animal expresses itself in varying ways, in ways that differentiate it from all of its other animal counterparts. These differences can be understood in the same way that human idiosyncrasies are accounted for through this age-old study of the stars and planets.

The more time an animal spends with a human, the more clearly the animal's personality is defined, and the easier it is to distinguish its salient character traits. Besides humans, animals also have a place in the universe's grand plan; the influence of the astrological signs over our pets is just as pronounced as it is with people.

When we know the sign under which our pet was born, we are better able to understand their tendencies and idiosyncrasies; we can then be more tolerant and, hopefully, more patient and loving toward the animal beings who share our space. When we learn that it is the influence of the signs and planets that work through each and every one of us—including the animals—we can appreciate the wondrous diversity of nature. By understanding how astrology affects all of the Earth's inhabitants, we are more equipped to act according to the immutable laws of the Universe and accept our fellow earth mates for who and what they are—quirks and all!

The purpose of this book is to help the pet owner "fine tune" his understanding of his animal companion—no matter the species. In a very simple way, astrology allows the reader to delve into the "psyche" of his pet, to perceive the existence of a legitimate "individual," packaged with its own personality, thoughts, feelings and idiosyncrasies.

An Aries rabbit, for example, will have the same basic personality tendencies as an Aries person: likely, it will be very independent, somewhat aggressive, and have an abundance of energy. Yes, an Aries rabbit!

Keep in mind, however, that an Aries rabbit will act out being an Aries in *rabbit* ways! An Aries horse will not toss its alfalfa bowl around in a fury the way an Aries rabbit will! Nor does it thump its back "paws" to show that it's angry.

If you're not sure which astrological sign your rabbit, bird, dog, cat or horse (or any other animal) was born under, read the following checklists for each individual sign, which is designed to help you "zero in" on your pet's astrological sign. More than likely, the animal will be true to its sign.

If you already know your pet's astrological sign, you're ahead of the game. Simply look up the sign and prepare yourself for a surprising experience. Animals and people are not so different after all.

When you discover your pet's astrological sign, not only will you understand its idiosyncrasies a lot better, you'll also have a better idea of how to deal with your pet on a psychological level. Say you have a Gemini cat. Knowing this, you may be more tolerant of his whimsical, neurotic tendencies, and indulge him by allowing him, (at times) to run through your house screaming.

Never expect more from your pet than he or she can naturally deliver. Allow the influence of the planets to work through him or her in the way in which your animal most naturally harmonizes with the universe— the way in which your pet was intended to express itself.

Identifying Your Pet's Astrological Sign

EVEN IF YOU don't know when your pet was born, it's not difficult to figure out its astrological sign. The following pages have been designed for you to determine your pet's sun sign. Go through the list of traits and tendencies listed for each sign, and check the items that most closely characterize your pet. The sign for which you indicate a majority (twelve or more) of similarities to your pet will more than likely tell you that that is your pet's astrological sign.

If it comes down to two signs, skip ahead and read the characterizations for those signs in the next section of this book. Then choose the one that most likely reflects your animal's behavior.

Is My Pet an ARIES?

My pet...

- ☐ has an enormous amount of energy.
- ☐ would prefer to be alone than to associate with other animals.
- ☐ is very insistent on what it wants and outwardly expresses it.
- ☐ often hits or cuts its head, or gets burrs or thistles in the head area.
- ☐ often projects its head forward or makes unnecessary motions with its head.
- ☐ does not always obey me or is difficult to discipline.
- ☐ bleeds easily.
- ☐ has a reddish hue to its skin tone or fur that is not necessarily characteristic of its species or breed.

- ☐ enjoys fighting with other animals and is known to instigate fights.
- ☐ has bitten me more than once.
- ☐ is always very enthusiastic or excitable.
- ☐ loves to break away from the "home front," often running non-stop.
- ☐ is very alert.
- ☐ has a bad temper.
- ☐ doesn't sleep much.
- ☐ has an overall personality that is quite aggressive.
- ☐ tends to be very impatient.
- ☐ is very impulsive, often moving or jumping up abruptly.
- ☐ is loud and boisterous.
- ☐ enjoys running (or galloping, hopping, slithering, etc.) forcefully, non-stop.

Is My Pet a TAURUS?

My pet...

- ☐ is extremely stubborn.
- ☐ has a larger than average neck.
- ☐ gravitates to creature comforts like blankets, pillows, soft bedding.
- ☐ is quite docile.
- ☐ moves rather slowly, in comparison to other animals of the same breed or species.
- ☐ rarely shows big displays of emotion.
- ☐ does not have a great amount of energy.
- ☐ is very patient.
- ☐ has a determined way in his or her overall manner. This is noticeable mostly in the way he or she moves.

- [ ] is sensual; it loves to be caressed and fondled, but more so, in a physical rather than emotional way.

- [ ] is loyal; even though his or her facial expression or gestures may not show it, is always by my side, steadfast and true.

- [ ] seems to subconsciously gravitate to things that are pretty.

- [ ] has a temper, even though he or she is not violent.

- [ ] has a broader (or more square) than average face.

- [ ] sometimes makes it difficult for me to assume what kind of mood he or she is in.

- [ ] loves music (other than rap or hard rock).

- [ ] tends to sleep a great deal.

- [ ] is relatively sociable.

- [ ] loves to eat.

- [ ] prefers to stay home, but welcomes the opportunity to go out for short periods.

Is My Pet a GEMINI?

My pet...

- ☐ "talks" a lot (barks, meows, chirps, sings, screams, cackles, grunts...or talks!).

- ☐ is very active.

- ☐ is not very emotional.

- ☐ enjoys learning new tricks and tends to learn them quickly.

- ☐ has a hard time keeping still; he or she is either continuously fidgeting, twitching, scratching or just nervously moving about.

- ☐ has a "sense of humor." Really seems to be humorous and likes to engage others in the fun.

- ☐ has a relatively short attention span.

- ☐ weighs on the thin side.

- ☐ has a longer than average head and neck.
- ☐ has very expressive, sparkling eyes.
- ☐ is often "changeable" in his or her affections; my pet is not constant in the way he or she responds to me.
- ☐ has a quick temper.
- ☐ is very agile.
- ☐ sometimes reminds me of a "circus dog."
- ☐ acts somewhat like a trickster. Sometimes I think my pet is actually trying to pull something over on me!
- ☐ is very mischievous.
- ☐ is extremely curious.
- ☐ has a variety of interests; flits from one activity to another within very short time periods.
- ☐ seems to run on nervous energy.
- ☐ does not have a big appetite.

HOLD BOTH HANDLES

Is My Pet a CANCER?

My pet...

- [ ] would rather stay home than roam around the neighborhood.

- [ ] is very attached to me.

- [ ] is very loving and attentive to me.

- [ ] seems to need a lot of affection and attention from me.

- [ ] gains weight easily.

- [ ] often vomits or appears to have an upset stomach.

- [ ] feels secure in having different things around her or him (e.g. toys, blankets).

- [ ] sometimes doesn't walk or get around easily.

- [ ] is an extremely good mother (even my male Cancer pet seems extraordinarily nurturing).

- ☐ is very gentle and kind.
- ☐ seems to be quite intuitive, often perceiving my thoughts or plans.
- ☐ tends to be a bit lazy.
- ☐ is often moody, changing from one mood to another within a relatively short time.
- ☐ does not always respond favorably to animals or people it doesn't know.
- ☐ favors the kitchen, especially.
- ☐ enjoys being in and around water.
- ☐ loves children (either its own, those of other animals, or even humans!).
- ☐ is very quiet.
- ☐ loves to eat.
- ☐ does not usually like to sleep or rest on a hard surface.

Is My Pet a LEO?

My pet...

- [ ] acts as if he or she is in charge of the household; can be quite domineering.

- [ ] has robust health.

- [ ] has a very strong, protective instinct.

- [ ] has a very big ego.

- [ ] appears to strut when walking, hopping, etc.

- [ ] thrives on attention and praise.

- [ ] is very good at defending him or herself.

- [ ] has a very strong, intense personality.

- [ ] is extremely faithful to me and all the members of my family.

- [ ] is loving in a "big-hearted" way. Is very openly affectionate without being sappy or coy.

- [ ] is very emotionally and psychologically secure.

- [ ] will fight only if he or she feels that it is necessary; not an animal that fights simply for the fun of it.

- [ ] is jealous of affection shown to other animals—or people!

- [ ] has charisma.

- [ ] is always happy.

- [ ] seems to have an inexhaustible amount of energy.

- [ ] is sometimes an actor; he or she acts flamboyantly or dramatically in order to get adulation, sympathy or some kind of attention.

- [ ] has a bad temper when provoked.

- [ ] is vociferous.

- [ ] expresses emotions openly.

Is My Pet a VIRGO?

My pet...

- ☐ is extremely clean.
- ☐ is naturally neat, orderly and tidy.
- ☐ gets very easily "annoyed."
- ☐ is very finicky about the food he or she eats.
- ☐ is very intelligent.
- ☐ is conniving.
- ☐ enjoys learning new tricks, and learns them quickly.
- ☐ is always anxious to please me.
- ☐ is often edgy or nervous.
- ☐ is not very affectionate; will bestow "just enough," and then go on his or her way to take care of more important things.

- ☐ is often somewhat melancholy.
- ☐ can be quite irritable for the slightest reason.
- ☐ is very versatile; has a lot of varied interests and always likes to be "busy."
- ☐ has a body that is somewhat rigid or inflexible.
- ☐ has had or tends to have intestinal trouble.
- ☐ can be selfish; does not take to sharing toys, possessions or food with anyone.
- ☐ is somewhat independent.
- ☐ would rather stay at home than go out.
- ☐ generally ignores the other animals in the household (where applicable).
- ☐ does not usually fuss when being groomed, or when having his or her nails/feathers trimmed.

Is My Pet a LIBRA?

My pet...

- ☐ is unusually good-looking for its species or breed.

- ☐ has a refined and pleasant manner.

- ☐ is a master at the art of persuasion; he can charmingly wrap me around his paw, claw, finger or hoof to get what he wants.

- ☐ does not like to fight.

- ☐ is very vociferous, and the noises my pet makes (bark, chirp, meow, etc.) are quite mellifluous.

- ☐ is self-indulgent; enjoys the good things in life. My pet likes to eat tasty food as well as to always be comfortable and content.

- ☐ is not very active physically.

- ☐ is usually relaxed and easy-going.
- ☐ has a well-proportioned body.
- ☐ has feathers, fur, hair or scales which are particularly sleek and fine in texture.
- ☐ does not drink much water.
- ☐ is affectionate, but fickle. His or her loyalties to me are not all that steadfast.
- ☐ moves very gracefully.
- ☐ usually gets along well with other animals and people.
- ☐ is very sociable.
- ☐ does not have sturdy health.
- ☐ is even-tempered.
- ☐ likes to share my company—just not too closely.
- ☐ is somewhat lazy.
- ☐ does not like to be alone.

Is My Pet a SCORPIO?

My pet...

- ☐ has very deep-set, penetrating eyes.

- ☐ is usually quiet and still.

- ☐ has a body relatively small to its species or breed.

- ☐ often seems to analyze or observe situations without reacting.

- ☐ rarely gets angry, but when the occasion arises, he or she can be vicious.

- ☐ is somewhat distant emotionally.

- ☐ is very determined; when it sets its mind on doing something, nothing can divert its attention.

- ☐ does not necessarily like the company of other animals.

- ☐ is sometimes hard to understand; he or she seems to be kind of mysterious.

- ☐ has a very intense and magnetic personality.
- ☐ is unusually active sexually (or at least seems to have the inclination).
- ☐ is very stubborn.
- ☐ has a prominent nose (relative to its species or breed).
- ☐ has, I feel, some kind of unusual inner strength or power.
- ☐ is not only intelligent; is quite sly or clever.
- ☐ learns quickly and thoroughly; however, he will carry out any request or "house rule" on his own terms and in his own time.
- ☐ is very independent.
- ☐ is devious or manipulative.
- ☐ always seems to be watching everything very closely.
- ☐ seems annoyed by the presence of other animals.

Is My Pet a SAGITTARIUS?

My pet...

- ☐ is very healthy.
- ☐ has strong, long legs (where applicable).
- ☐ is very physically active.
- ☐ would rather roam than stay at home.
- ☐ seems to have an endless amount of energy.
- ☐ is noble.
- ☐ is always in a good mood.
- ☐ is not quick to pick a fight, although he or she will get angry if provoked.
- ☐ is quite vociferous.

- ☐ has a short attention span, gets bored easily; he is constantly looking for something different to do.

- ☐ is affectionate—but only for short spurts of time.

- ☐ is fearless; he is not afraid to take a risk or do something daring.

- ☐ would rather stay outside than inside.

- ☐ is curious.

- ☐ is often very restless.

- ☐ is, for the most part, very obedient.

- ☐ is very mischievous.

- ☐ is always ready "to go" someplace, any place.

- ☐ is often difficult to control.

Is My Pet a CAPRICORN?

My pet...

- ☐ is stingy and possessive with its things and its food.
- ☐ is "petty."
- ☐ is extremely intelligent.
- ☐ has a manipulative bent to his or her personality.
- ☐ never gets sick; if so, it recovers quickly and completely.
- ☐ is not very active.
- ☐ is usually quiet and reclusive.
- ☐ is cold, inexpressive and generally inhibited.
- ☐ is never mischievous or daring.
- ☐ has a hard time bonding with anyone—animals or humans.

- [ ] does not like to play or socialize with other animals.
- [ ] does not like to play, for the most part.
- [ ] is very bony.
- [ ] moves rather slowly.
- [ ] has tooth problems.
- [ ] would rather be inside than outside.
- [ ] walks and generally moves with a certain amount of caution.
- [ ] is usually depressed.
- [ ] has skin problems.
- [ ] has an angular (or square) face, despite its breed or species.

ENTER AT YOUR OWN RISK

Is My Pet an AQUARIUS?

My pet...

- ☐ is extremely independent.
- ☐ is particularly striking/good looking.
- ☐ has virtually no attention span.
- ☐ often moves about nervously and aimlessly.
- ☐ is very vivacious.
- ☐ is friendly to everyone, but in a very superficial way.
- ☐ would rather be outside than inside.
- ☐ is insecure, often not acting with confidence or certainty.
- ☐ is erratic, excitable and/or neurotic.
- ☐ usually seems to be happy, even though he or she seems to have bouts of depression from time to time.

- [ ] sometimes seems to be "scatter-brained."
- [ ] rarely stays still.
- [ ] is good-natured.
- [ ] likes to socialize with people and other animals.
- [ ] runs mostly on nervous energy.
- [ ] tends to have weak or pronounced ankles (where applicable).
- [ ] is extremely sensitive; he or she is emotionally unstable.
- [ ] is skittish and insecure.
- [ ] does not like the dark.
- [ ] likes to "cuddle up" next to or near electrical appliances or wires (where applicable).

Is My Pet a PISCES?

My pet...

☐ is extraordinarily gentle.

☐ seems to sense my thoughts and feelings.

☐ has a mystical quality; seems to be much more than just a "dog," "cat," "rabbit," "bird," "pig," "iguana," etc. (whatever applies here).

☐ is very affectionate.

☐ would rather be inside than outside.

☐ lovingly tolerates the other pets in the household, but prefers not to engage in boisterous activity.

☐ sleeps a lot.

☐ loves to cuddle up next to me.

☐ is quiet; never makes any noise.

- ☐ has a very good temperament. Never gets angry or "out of sorts."

- ☐ has rather weak health.

- ☐ has fur, feathers, or hair that is fine and somewhat sparse or thin.

- ☐ does not have a strong walk, trot or hop.

- ☐ is totally devoted to me.

- ☐ is regularly depressed or "down in the dumps."

- ☐ and I seem to have a psychic bond.

- ☐ does not seem to be too emotionally stable or confident.

- ☐ has (or has had) problems with its feet or lungs; he or she gets colds often.

- ☐ loves to be in or around water.

- ☐ likes to hide under furniture or in secluded places.

Your Pet's Sign

THE FOLLOWING SECTION provides you with general and specific analyses of animals' personalities, physical characteristics, health issues, and likes and dislikes, based on the sign of the zodiac under which the animal was born. Animals often behave, respond, think and emote in ways that are uncannily similar to humans. Astrology is a marvelously helpful tool for enabling us to understand and appreciate our animal companions.

As you read about your pet's personality traits and idiosyncracies, pay particularly close attention to the infomation regarding your pet's health and body type so you can better deal with your pet's physical, and emotional, well-being.

Your ARIES Pet
(March 21–April 19)

Whether you have a dog, a cat, a bird, or even a ferret or a duck, your Aries pet will be more aggressive than those born under almost any other sign. They will have lots of energy, but might burn out quickly; thus your Aries Golden Retriever may play "retrieve the ball" for a lot shorter time than, say, your Sagittarian Dalmatian!

When your pet is born under the sign of Aries, it will never be reticent in pushing its weight around and letting any other pets know that he, or she, is first in line. More often than not, your Aries pet will want to be the only one in line! Aries animals usually prefer to be the only pet in the household, and can be quite raucous if there is any kind of competition. Of course, an Aries Labrador Retriever might not mind a nice, juicy, slow-footed duck around the house to sink his teeth into for an occasional hors d'oeuvre. But when it comes down to sharing, forget it; these guys are selfish—with their toys, their food, their master.

Be very careful of fights when you have an Aries pet around. Aries rabbits can be just as aggressive as an Aries bulldog. (I'd keep the bulldog away from the rabbit.) Whatever your animal does to show that it wants attention or food, or that it's angry (either by pecking, screeching, scratching, barking or biting), an Aries animal will express it spontaneously, aggressively and powerfully. Don't encourage aggressive behavior; Aries animals love to fight, and once they start, it's almost impossible to get them to stop. Since Aries rules the head, your Aries pet will more than likely use that part of the body when showing any type of aggression. Where cats are often known to "bat" with their paws, your Aries cat may be the one that "rams" its head into you or some other unsuspecting animal.

Try to avoid having more than one Aries pet at a time—especially if they are pets that intermingle, such as pets of the same species. They may get along great for the most part, enjoying the abundant energy of the other; but when that full moon rises, any pet can turn into a werewolf, even though an Aries is more likely to do so than those of most other signs. Remember that Aries are very physical; therefore, it is not unusual for them to pick a fight from time to time.

Being very physical, Aries animals are extremely energetic and active. They enjoy different kinds of physical interaction (not just fighting). They happen to like sex a lot, too. Aries pets are the most likely to run off (or fly off), so be sure to keep them safe and secured in your yard or home.

Since Aries rules the head, occasionally check their teeth, gums, eyes, nose, ears and general head area for any unusual ailments. Be sure to keep your Aries companion out of extreme heat. Being a fire sign, Aries animals are more susceptible to rashes and heat-induced problems, especially in the summertime.

Aries need lots of exercise, particularly in a large, open area where they can run, fly, gallop or hop freely and happily. Enclosing an Aries animal is like giving it a prison sentence. If your pet must be enclosed, see to it that its enclosure allows the animal lots of movement, and allow it to move about outside the enclosure as often as possible.

Your TAURUS Pet
(April 20–May 20)

If you want an easy-going, stay-at-home, mild-mannered pet, try a Taurus. The only real downside to a Taurean dog, cat, horse, or whatever, is that they tend to be really stubborn. It's also more than likely that this animal will wait for you to approach him than for him to go to you. Call them for as long as you like; repeat their name fifty times; scream at them, beg them, be nice to them. They won't come until they feel like it. They really like to stay where they are, and have others visit them or tend to them. And on that note, once you get to wherever they may be snoozing or luxuriating (a typical Taurean trait), they will always expect some kind of service—like a back rub or some special treat that they can s-l-o-w-l-y munch on.

Yes, Taurus is somewhat slow...in almost every respect. They take life easily. Your Taurus cat can sit longer than any other, contemplating a picture on the wall of the Three Blind Mice. Your Taurus dog doesn't have to go anywhere—often for hours—to feel content and totally at peace. Your Taurus horse will have no problem standing in its stable all week until you decide to drag him or her out for a reluctant trot around the track or block. This is why Taurus makes a great traveling companion. They love to sit in the car (this usually does not pertain to horses) while you chauffeur them anywhere. Just make sure to take plenty of comfy blankets and pillows for them to sprawl out on during the ride. Being an earth sign, the Taurus influence will make your pet much less active than an Aries. The Taurean animal isn't very energetic, and prefers to just "hang out" and luxuriate, rather than jump through hoops, chase squirrels, gallop a marathon or play Frisbee ad nauseam. This is not to say that they have no energy at all; they actually have quite a bit, but the nature of Taurus is such that it expends its energy conservatively.

Taurus is ruled by the planet Venus, so your pet will be inclined to behave in "Venusian" ways: they like to feel "comfy"; they like to be groomed, pampered, catered to. They lap it all up, and when you think you're all done "pampering" them, they think you've just begun. Taurean cats love to be rubbed and caressed. Their sensuous purrs will tell you just how much they appreciate all the attention you're giving them (even though they expect it). If your pet was born under the sign of Taurus the Bull, no matter what species it is, it will love to be groomed. Shampoo it, condition it, brush it, comb it, rub it, clip it, shave it, primp it—just don't ignore it—and your pet will love it. You'll think that your pet is "so good," and "so patient"; but all he or she is thinking is, "I don't ever want this to end. Keep doing it to me."

Make sure you have lots of cuddly things for your Taurus pet, like soft blankets, cushy pillows and beds, and make sure that everything you supply them with is pretty. Don't forget, we're talking about Venus here. These animals are very aesthetically inclined—and you don't have to be human for Taurus's fine-tuned sense of beauty to cast down its influence. If you have a bird, put a mirror in its cage so it can primp, pose and flex, all the while admiring its Taurean beauty. These animals may not consciously be aware that they are actually attracted to beauty, but the natural Venusian quality of their being automatically attracts them to it. They really do know—somehow—when they are around beauty and when they are not. Of all my shoes that Rosebud, my Taurean Fox Terrier, could have chosen to chew on, she chose my pale pink pumps with a bow—my prettiest pair of shoes!

Taurus rules the neck and throat. This makes that area of your pet's body particularly sensitive or vulnerable to kinks, sore throats, colds, coughs, pulled muscles, and the like. Be sure not to use a choke chain when you are not walking your dog, and keep all collars comfortable around your Taurean pet's neck. Regularly check to make sure that it's not too tight; tightness can change due to weight gain or fur growth.

While on the subject of "weight gain," Taureans are so inclined, so watch your pet's diet, and avoid the temptation to feed them table scraps and junk food. They gain weight very easily. Also avoid giving them meat and chicken bones as these can lodge in their most sensitive area—their throats.

Overall, your Taurean pet should be a comforting companion (or it could be the other way around). They are easy to train, they welcome any nice gesture you want to do for them, and they are more likely than not to stay around the home front, not straying too far from all the luxuries of their abode.

Your
GEMINI Pet
(May 21–June 20)

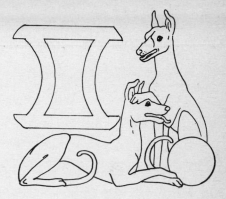

If you're a Gemini yourself, you may have an array of different animals. Gemini likes variety, so your pets will, too. The greatest punishment you can do to your Gemini pet is to isolate it. They love to have friends, to mingle and to socialize. Always have a large variety of toys and provide your Gemini snake, rabbit, iguana, dog, cat or guinea pig with lots of entertainment. (Just make sure the snake's entertainment isn't the guinea pig!)

Gemini people like to talk a lot; so do Gemini animals, but in their own language. A Gemini dog will bark a lot more than a Taurus dog; Gemini birds love to sing, chirp, cackle or shriek all day long to their heart's content. Your Gemini parrot will have a much larger than average vocabulary, and will talk incessantly. Geminis love noise. They also like constant activity, but different kinds of activity—and often all at the same time! So, your Gemini cat might indulge in batting a bell for five minutes, then move on to batting the dog's tail for another three, then she'll easily get bored with the whole "batting" scene and roll around for awhile, until she gets the urge to watch TV next to you on the sofa for about ten seconds. Or your Gemini parakeet may like to sing, push its bell, look at itself in the mirror and sway from side to side—all at the same time!

Besides being verbose, your Gemini pet is also quite mental; it's not unusual for this creature to be extremely astute and to catch on very quickly to what you want it to do. They actually enjoy learning a variety of tricks and commands; often it's not surprising to see a Gemini animal merely observe something that a human does, and then imitate the act—*purrfectly!* I once had a Gemini German Shepherd, who observed me turn on the water faucet outside—once. A few days later, when he found his water bowl empty, guess what Thor did. Unfortunately, he never learned to turn the water off!

A Gemini animal will rarely get bored if he or she has a variety of things to do all hours of the day. Many times they function purely on nervous energy—humans do not have a monopoly on neurosis! Because of this abundance of nervous energy that your Gemini pets probably possess, it is of utmost importance that they get enough rest and that their sleeping quarters be conducive to "good sleep." Make sure that the slightest disruptions can be avoided. Snoozing is like aspirin for a Gemini pet's agitated nervous system.

Most animals perceive the world through their noses. Gemini animals have an extremely fine-tuned sense of smell. Dogs who work for the police to track down people, drugs, weapons or any kind of contraband probably have a strong Gemini influence for them to have such keen olfactory functioning. Your Gemini pet's five senses will all be very acute. Their hearing will be extraordinarily sharp, their eyesight will be better than those of other signs within their species, and their eyes will often sparkle.

Your Gemini pet will be particularly finicky when it comes to food; taste is another sense with which Geminis are particularly sensitive. Give your Gemini cat, dog or rabbit very tasty food, and often add variety to your pet's diet. (In the case of dogs, don't vary it too much. Your canine's Gemini nature will take well to a little something different every now and then, but don't overdo it.)

Touch is a sense that your Gemini pet can probably do without. They are not very tactile, and probably won't invite you to pet them too often. Geminis are so sensitive to touch that your companion animal born under this sign may flinch or recoil at your slightest stroke or pat. Their systems are highly nervous, so don't take this typical Gemini reaction personally; it's just the nature of the beast!

Gemini actually rules the nervous system, as well as the arms and the shoulders. So unless your pet happens to be a primate (or any other animal with arms and shoulders), you only need be concerned about your pet's nervous system. If you do have a monkey or chimpanzee, make sure he or she keeps his arms and hands out of dangerous places like garbage disposals, or doesn't swing too much to the point of dislocating his or her shoulder! And, by all means, do not offer coffee to your Gemini primate (or to *any* animal, for that matter); it will really do a number on his already very fragile nervous system! For all the rest of us who have Gemini animal companions that have only legs, make sure that the food you feed your pets does not affect their nervous system—especially food with sugar (which should *never* be given to any pet). Don't agitate your Gemini pet; they are already somewhat agitated by nature, so train or play with your pet without stressing him out. Certainly they need a lot of variety and excitement, but they also require high degrees of tranquillity and balance.

Your
CANCER Pet
(June 21–July 23)

If the idea of referring to your pet as a "Cancer" bothers you, then try "Moon Child." The sign of Cancer the Crab is also known as the Moon Children because this sign is ruled by the moon.

When the moon is full, people often act out of the ordinary, or they at least *feel* out of the ordinary. People are more ornery, aggressive, passionate and violent during a full moon. We already know how the moon affects the water on our planet. There's nothing more violent than tumultuous waves at high tide—all because of the moon.

Did you ever observe your pet on a full moon? Animals are much more in tune with nature than we humans could ever imagine being. (Consider their restlessness, hours—or even days—before a major earthquake.) Everyone, including animals, reacts in some way or another to the moon. Imagine, then, how sensitive to this satellite of ours are those who are born under its influence—i.e. the Moon Children.

Be particularly observant of your Moon Child dog, cat or iguana on Mondays. Most people are out of sorts on the "day of the Moon," and animals are no exception. Your pet may be more depressed, more "whiny," more needy of your attention or affection. And if there's a full moon on any Monday, be particularly sensitive and aware of your companion's intense mood swings. Don't make demands on your Cancer pet or expect it to respond favorably when the Moon is doing a number on its children.

The most emotional and sensitive (except for Pisces) of all your pets will be your Cancer the Crab. Even though your pet may not be an actual crab, the influence of Cancer will certainly make your dog, parrot, monkey or kitty cat awfully crabby at times—and probably even more so on a full moon.

Your Cancer pet will be a very affectionate member of the zodiacal zoo, regularly licking you, cooing, cuddling up to you; but he or she will also require much affection from you. Be sure to provide them with as much love and tenderness as you can muster—full moon or not! The attention you give to a Cancer dog is not the same as you would give to a Gemini dog. Gemini dogs need mental stimulation and lots of physical activity. Moon Children, on the other hand, need plenty of "quiet time," massages, kisses, and lots of reassurance that you adore them. They are extremely needy emotionally, and this should not be taken lightly; being as sensitive as they are, Cancer animals will quickly pick up any resentment or anger you may be harboring. Constant emotional gratification is what these special creatures need.

If you are deciding between a pet that you know was born under the sign of Cancer and another one that was born under, say Sagittarius, and you know you won't be spending much time at home, take the Sagittarian! Cancer pets, being so "clingy" and emotionally needy, are much happier knowing that you're there, close by, in case they may need an occasional "pat" of reassurance that they're safe and, more importantly, that they are loved. Talk to them gently and shower them with lots of T.L.C.

Speaking of showers, they probably wouldn't mind a bath or a shower now and then; Cancer is a water sign, and any chance they get to go swimming, take a run (a gentle run) on the beach, or maybe even take a shower or bath would please a Moon Pet quite well.

Your Cancer pet will probably enjoy the company of other pets—especially the younger ones. Cancers like to mother, even if they are male. The case in which a cat nursed a baby squirrel back to health is a perfect example of the Cancerian influence at work. If you don't have younger pets for your older Cancer pets to care for, provide them with a small, stuffed animal that can feed your Moon Animal's mothering instincts.

All your pets' diets should be carefully watched to provide them with the most balanced and nutritious foods available. Since the sign of Cancer rules the stomach, extra special attention should be given to the food you give to your Moon Pet. They are particularly vulnerable to ulcers, upset stomachs, vomiting, and any other disorders that may affect the alimentary canal and the stomach area.

Cancer pets like to stay at home; so, like the Taurus, you shouldn't have any problem keeping these Moon Children indoors. As long as you're there, and they feel well taken care of and loved, everything in a Cancerian animal's world is complete. Just don't be too surprised if, on a full moon, these seemingly innocent critters turn into werewolves!

Your LEO Pet
(July 23–August 22)

Your Leo animal companion resembles the Cancerian in one major respect: he or she requires a lot of affection. But instead of whining or gentle nudging for some T.L.C., Leo the Lion *demands* it! In a very cat-like way (even if you have a monkey, dog or horse), your Leo pet will very subtly and seductively indicate to you that a back rub is just what it needs. So how do they do that seductive routine? With their eyes: those alluring, begging eyes, that say, "Oh, won't you please give me a back rub. I do so need one—right now." Or they express it with their body movements; a Leo doesn't need to be a cat to act like one. A Leo dog can communicate in as much of a seductive way as a cat, swaying back and forth, coquettishly tossing its head over its shoulder, throwing you a "come hither" look.

When your Leo pet wants something, whether it's a back rub, a cookie or a "walkie-walkie," he or she will let you know in an assertive, yet ingratiating manner. Their way is catlike, but it's also elegant, regal and commanding. So, whenever your pet wants something, he or she will do whatever it takes to get it...usually by putting on a great Academy Award-winning performance.

Leos are the show-offs—the actors—of the zodiac, and your Leo pet is probably no exception. Leo dogs prance, Leo cats strut, Leo rabbits raise their head in a lofty manner, and Leo birds jut out their chests as if to say: "I'm very important."

Your Leo pet is not needy like your Cancer pet may be. Oh, no; these astrological lions are very secure. Remember, they are well aware that their purpose is to protect you. They are fearless and fierce, but a little conceited as well. You might just say that they have a very healthy ego. Just don't ever wound it!

When they are not in the mood for something (say, a bath), you'll definitely know it. Leo pulls no punches. They have a temper. They can turn that charismatic charm on and off at will, and let you know who's really the boss. (After all, they are the King of Beasts.) They will "fight 'til the death" if they feel they have to. They are tenacious in everything they do, and they won't stop until they get their way.

As with all royalty, your Leo pet is no exception when it comes to requiring an abundance of praise, recognition and adoration. Shower your furry, feathery or scaly beast with loads of compliments. Praise their every trick with superlative words and their favorite yummy treats.

The tenacity of Leo isn't always necessarily negative. You won't find a ferret, iguana, dog, cat or bird that's more loyal than a Leo. They will defend you, respect you and be your faithful companion for life. But, remember that word, "respect"; that's a biggie for all Leos—human or animal. Of course, all living beings must be respected; but the Leo demands it. If you're out of line with your Leo pet, he or she will let you know in no uncertain terms. For a Leo, adulation, loyalty and total devotion to you are not unconditional and do not come free.

The sign of Leo rules the heart, the spine and the back. This makes Leo animals more vulnerable to weak hearts, heart attacks, and disorders related to the back and spine areas. Leos are, however, extremely hardy, and rarely suffer major health problems, especially when they are well taken care of.

If you have more than one animal in your household, and one is a Leo, make sure that "one" is allowed to be the leader of the pack. If you've got two Leos, you might encounter a problem. Leos are natural born leaders—and they know it. They make great watch dogs, but don't just toss them outside and leave them there to guard your house without plenty of respectful love and attention from your end. They defend their post as dogmatically as they defend you. But underneath all that bravado, their heart is every bit as tender as that of a pussycat.

Your
VIRGO Pet
(August 23– September 22)

You won't have to worry about your place (or your pet's) being in order when your pet is a Virgo. They are extremely neat, clean and tidy; nature just made them that way. Everything this pet does—from walking, eating, drinking and sleeping to caring for their beds, blankets, pillows and toys—is done in a very orderly, meticulous, neat and quiet manner. You'll hardly know they're around.

Rover or Trixie won't ask much of you, just some nutritious food (they are quite finicky about what they eat) and a comfortable place to rest when they're not busy putting their toys away or straightening up their bed. Virgo pets, like Virgo people, always have to be busy doing something; if not, they feel helpless and bored. Give your Virgo pet something practical to do as often as possible; teach him or her some tricks that can be useful, such as bringing in the newspaper, switching on the lights when it gets dark, or getting their own food when they're hungry. Virgos are extremely intelligent, very quick to learn, and have a terrific memory. No matter what you teach your self-sufficient Virgo companion, you'll never have to worry about their forgetting what you taught them.

Your Virgo pet will be more than delighted to be of service to you. Whatever is your wish will be his or her command. Virgo is the sign of service, so it will be your pet's natural tendency to desire to follow through with whatever command you ask of him. Their motto is "eager to please."

Sometimes you may find your Virgo pet somewhat ornery. The Virgo energy can make humans and animals cranky. In the case of your Virgo pets, they could snap or get annoyed at trivial things. This is not necessarily a typical way of being for Virgo animals, but if your pet does get this way from time to time, just write it off as a harmless Virgoan idiosyncrasy. For the most part, your Virgo pet should behave almost like an angel, always anxious to comply with your wishes and to not get in anybody's way.

Animals are, by nature, very clean beings, always grooming and cleaning themselves and maintaining relatively neat and clean surroundings. Virgos invented the words "neat" and "clean;" so help them out when they need it. Make sure your Virgo bunny's hutch is regularly cleaned out, that he or she uses a litter box with clean shavings at all times. Make sure your Virgo bird's water and food are always fresh, and be sure that his cage is always up to Virgo standards. Of course, all animals' things should be clean and well taken care of; but the Virgo animal will be particularly picky, and will let you know, in some way, if things are not in order. One Virgo rabbit I knew used to actually throw his litter box and turn it upside down when it got too dirty for his taste.

Virgo rules the intestines as well as the nervous system. Be particularly careful with the food your Virgo pets eat. Offer them acidophilus or yogurt often. The live cultures in these foods will keep their sensitive innards functioning smoothly and regularly. Dogs, cats and rabbits alike love acidophilus and yogurt, and it's so good for them. Check with your veterinarian if you have other kinds of animals.

Like Gemini, Virgo also rules the nervous system; so it's not uncommon for your Virgo pet to get a bit edgy or agitated—especially when he or she has nothing to do! Deprive any Virgo of an agenda, and they'll use up a lot of nervous energy doing nothing, except maybe chewing on their nails or being testy with you or your other pets. Besides having what to do, your Virgo pet needs plenty of sleep. No other sign, other than Gemini, needs as much sleep as Virgo; sleep for a Virgo is like the oil that keeps their nervous systems from getting rusty.

Don't get offended if your Virgo pet seems a bit more independent than you might like. As much as it wants to please you, it also expects some free time alone. So don't be concerned if Spot or Pierre pick a clean remote corner to either take an afternoon snooze, or to just sit back and relax and watch all the action from afar. All they're doing is recharging their delicate systems so they can be bright-eyed, bushy-tailed and faithfully ready to serve their master (that's you) with that characteristically unerring Virgoan precision and unending devotion.

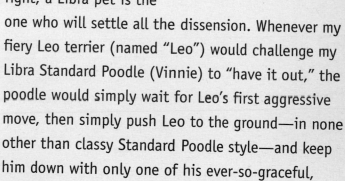

Your LIBRA Pet
(September 23– October 22)

If you've got pets in your house that constantly fight, a Libra pet is the one who will settle all the dissension. Whenever my fiery Leo terrier (named "Leo") would challenge my Libra Standard Poodle (Vinnie) to "have it out," the poodle would simply wait for Leo's first aggressive move, then simply push Leo to the ground—in none other than classy Standard Poodle style—and keep him down with only one of his ever-so-graceful, long, elegant, black paws. That is a typically Libran way to be: to make a point—but peaceably—and with class and strength.

No matter what species your animal companion is, if it's a Libra, it will do everything it can to keep the peace. Libras are not fighters; but, like Vinnie, they will sometimes take measures to insure that harmony on the homestead is properly and regularly maintained. It's hard to incite a Libran to fight; they'll usually just try to avoid a fight or stop one—and sometimes they have to be tough to pull it off. That's why your other pets (if you have any) will harbor a resentful respect for the Libran peacekeeper.

If you have no other pets, there can be a downside to that, too; that's because Libra thrives on companionship. If you're always home, then your Libra dog, cat, or "whatever" is perfectly content. They just need to know that someone is around, someone to love and someone to look after them. Venus, the planet of love and beauty, rules Libra. Therefore these loving—and lovely—creatures not only need love, they also require an object of love—someone like...you! Unlike the other Venus-ruled sign, Taurus, your Libra pet won't necessarily seek physical affection. And unlike Cancer animals, they won't be so emotionally needy or clinging. You won't hear much whimpering from a Libra like you might from a Cancer; Libra is more self-sufficient, as long as they know that they have a companion—somewhere. They don't necessarily need to have you near them all the time; they just need to know that they belong to you, and that they're part of the family.

Being an air sign, they'll be less tactile, less "earthy." That doesn't mean they wouldn't like a gentle back rub from time to time; but for the most part, Libras would just as soon be socializing with the other cats on the block or admiring some new toy that their owner could not resist buying for them. Don't expect your Libra pet to seek you out for a cuddling session. Although their emotional needs are high, they are usually met by simply sharing your company. Again, they're not into "touching" as much as relating. As long as your Libra pet is not left out, and she is made to feel that she's a part of what's going on, you'll have a perfectly content animal in the house.

Another thing about Libras: they are very attractive. Being ruled by the planet of love and beauty puts these Venusian creatures "one up" in the good looks bracket. Yet, it's not always looks that make your Libran companions so lovely; it could just be the way they stride or prance, the way they toss their locks, or their mellifluous chirp or howl. Whatever it is, a Libra animal is definitely an eye-catcher. Thus, your pet doesn't have to be an elegant Afghan Hound or a champion stallion to be rated "gorgeous." Even a Libran bulldog comes across as somewhat charming and alluring—at least to the bulldog opposite sex. Whatever the species or breed, Librans stand out as having a particular flair.

And, speaking of "charming," your Libra pet doesn't have to be a snake to be a charmer. They have a way of wrapping you around their paw, claw or hoof to get whatever they want. They can be so subtle that you won't even be aware of those manipulative, whimpering, soulful looks, or other charming attention-getting devices they'll throw your way. They have to feed that incessant Venusian need of theirs to be noticed or wanted;

they need this in order to always feel content and "balanced."

Since Libra rules the kidneys, make sure your Venus-ruled pet has plenty of clean, purified water at all times; encourage him or her to drink as often as possible in order to keep those kidneys in constant, tip-top shape.

Your SCORPIO Pet
(October 23– November 21)

Don't get discouraged if you feel you can't quite figure out your Scorpio pet. One minute they can be very seductive, brushing— oh, so sensually—up and down your leg; the next minute they can be utterly petulant! Your Scorpio pet won't be very easy to figure out if it is true to its sign. Just like their human counterparts, Scorpio animals have a certain mystique to them. They are very intense in their feelings, but you won't always be aware of it. When your companion Shitzu is miffed because you shooed her away, if she's a Scorpio, she won't show her hurt by whining or begging for attention. Oh, no. Instead, she may become withdrawn, aloof and as cold as ice. (Scorpio represents fixed water.) The only clue you'll get from this will be her fixed, impenetrable stare with those famous, intense, Scorpionic eyes. This is one animal that won't try to make up or smooth things over like most noble pets will. Just don't get too close if you've offended or reprimanded your Scorpio pet. You never know what plan of attack they may have up their shank. If another pet in your household has been annoying your Scorpio pet, the latter may tolerate this only so long, until one day, when it's least expected, Scorpio attacks—and the attack may be vicious.

Nonetheless, Scorpio pets generally show unswerving loyalty and devotion, the likes of which are rarely seen in animals born under any other sign, except maybe Leo. Scorpio is a fixed sign, and with it goes a fixed dedication to its owner. One interesting characteristic about these animals, however, is that if they feel betrayed or abused, they are known to either retaliate viciously or to simply ignore you. The Scorpio pet can often seem more human than any of their zodiacal relatives because of their petty, yet subtle, means of expressing their scorn. Scorpio, like Leo, demands respect; when that respect is disregarded, your pet doesn't have to be a scorpion to strike with its stinger.

Your Scorpio pet's feelings for you are so deep that you'll often do double-takes, wondering if there's a human somewhere inside that furry, feathery or scaly body. Don't ever think of giving this pet away; once it's devoted to one person, that's it for life! Scorpio pets, in particular, would have an extremely difficult time adapting to a different owner, let alone developing any kind of loyalty to him or her. Your Scorpio pet may differ from other pets in that they are less playful and more serious. They tend to be very observant of everything that's going on. You may not even realize that they're in the room; they are quiet and stealthy in their movements and overall behavior.

Another major characteristic that you might often see in your Scorpio pet is its possessiveness—with everything, including you. Don't allow any animal or human to play with its toys, lie in its bed, eat its food, or make any kind of overtures toward you! Where a Leo dog, for example, may growl or even just shove the intruder out of the way, your Scorpio pet could get vituperative or just plain mean. Scorpio pets can make wonderful companions as long as they are not provoked and no one gets in their way.

You may find that your Scorpio pet is not all that sociable. So, whether you have other pets or not, is really of no consequence to the somewhat snooty Scorpio. They are just as happy being on their own, being quietly vigilant of all the happenings in your home, making sure that no one interferes with what they consider to be theirs.

Scorpio rules the reproductive organs. Your Scorpio animal may appear to be more highly sexed than "normal," but, in actuality, this is normal for Scorpio. Even well into old age, you may see your seasoned Scorpio Doberman feel aroused every time he sees the prissy new Collie sail by. (She's an Aquarius, though, so she won't give him the time of day—although she may not have a choice!) As with all dogs, spaying and neutering is the safest way to avoid problems later on, and this is particularly so with those born under the sign of Scorpio.

Your
SAGITTARIUS
Pet

(November 22–December 21)

If you enjoy hiking, boating, running or any kind of outdoor activity with your four-legged canine pal, a Sagittarius is the one to have. If you have a Sag cat, it's going to be hard keeping it inside all the time—or even half the time. If you've got an animal that traditionally stays in cages, don't expect to have a real happy enclosed Sagittarian critter. ALL Sagittarians need freedom, openness, fresh air, and the ability to move around—a lot!

Sagittarius is the most physically active sign; therefore all its "members" must live according to their individual sign's requisites.

The more your Sagittarian pet can run, fly, slither, hop, trot or swim, the happier it will be. Limit your pet's physical activity as little as possible, as their physical and emotional well-being greatly depend on being able to be out and about and to roam freely.

Your relationship with this centaur should be quite healthy. What you see in this pet is exactly what you'll get; there are no Scorpio-type surprises or Leo-type pride hang-ups when you have a "true-to-form" Sagittarian for a pet. Your Sagittarius pet will be open and enthusiastic all the time; and, being born under a "mutable" sign, he or she will be flexible in going along with just about anything you'd like to do—especially if it has to do with moving about.

Because Sag animals are so adaptable and active, you'll have no problem taking them anywhere—in your car, boat, plane or RV. They've also got quite a sturdy constitution, so you won't have to worry about bringing along extra paper towels: they don't tend to get motion sickness.

Sagittarians have lots of energy, and rarely burn out. Even so, make sure your companion doesn't push it too far. Make sure they rest enough to keep that high energy level in optimal condition. Your Sagittarian pet should not have any health problems other than those they may "run into" while off on one of their adventures. Just be sure you know where they are at all times, and that danger in any form is nowhere near these innocent, child-like creatures. Sagittarians are known to be accident prone, so be sure to keep this in mind with regards to your somewhat careless and mischievous animal.

Your Sagittarian pet will be quite independent, so you won't have to worry if you're not there all the time; of course it would be nice if he had a friend to romp around with when you're nowhere to be found. They do tend to get rather bored when there's nothing to do. Your Sag pet is not the type to lie quietly, counting sheep or any other animal. The only thing they'll be counting on is having fun. Yes, this pet—which is represented by the centaur: half horse, half man—really does love to horse around. Any trouble they can get into, Sagittarians will be sure to find it. They are extremely playful and never seem to tire. Their energy supply is inexhaustible. Therefore, if you don't have the same type of Sagittarian stamina as your pet, you'd be doing your pet and yourself a great favor if you got her a friend. Of course try to make sure, in advance, that this "friend" is not a lethargic Cancerian type or a "not-too-swift" Taurean. A Gemini would be a nice playmate, so would an Aries, a Leo, or even another Sagittarius.

It is particularly important that your Sag companion be able to romp around as much as possible, since this sign rules the legs. If your pet happens to not have legs (as in the case of fish, snakes or seals), they still need a lot of exercise, and all the other Sagittarian traits still apply. Although their legs should be in top condition—strong and well-formed—watch your "legged" beast for possible ailments to those important appendages such as swelling, bruising, bone breakage or malformation. The norm, however, is that these animals are healthy overall, and that their legs are their strong point. This is particularly interesting since most parts of the body ruled by specific signs are rendered vulnerable and weak to those who are born under those signs. Not so for Sagittarians!

Your Sagittarian pet will be fun and fun-loving, playful, gregarious, "happy" and always active, rarely tiring of anything—except of doing nothing.

Your CAPRICORN Pet
(December 22–January 19)

You don't necessarily need to have a goat, per se, to have a "Capricorn pet," even though this particular sign of the zodiac is represented by none other than the goat. Your Capricorn pet will tend to be anything but capricious. There is nothing whimsical about dogs, cats, horses or parrots born under this sign. They are as steadfast and reliable as a goat is sure-footed. Even though, on the one hand, this might seem like a good deal, on the other, these very down-to-earth animals may be a bit dull. They're more likely to sit around and simply watch while your Gemini and Sagittarius cats tease and titillate each other. Your Capricorn pet is probably very serious...and takes life very seriously as well. Most importantly, he or she takes you very seriously. Although there probably won't be much fun and games with this animal, you can be sure that he or she will follow the rules right down to the last letter. Being extremely intelligent, the Capricorn pet will learn exactly what you want very quickly, and will do it with extreme pleasure. Capricorns are quite stoic; they thrive on duty and on what's "right." You won't have to worry about your Capricornian chimpanzee monkeying around or your cat being cantankerous or your dog being dogged. In fact, it's their obedience and sense of duty that makes your Capricorn pets so doggone boring.

But if you're the kind of pet owner who doesn't like surprises, who wants to know what your four-legged, two-legged or "legless" critter is up to...all the time, get yourself an animal born under the sign of the goat.

They'll learn all the tricks you teach them, and there won't be a single flaw in their performance. They may move a little slowly, but they are the masters of the old saying: "Better to be safe than sorry." Remember, these are sure-footed goats. No slip-ups while they're scaling that steep, icy precipice.

And, speaking of icy, your Capricorn pet isn't likely to be too warm or affectionate. Capricorn is a "rigid" (remember "stoic") sign; all members of its sign are influenced in this way. You'll have devotion and loyalty you can count on, obedience is a given, and A+ behavior is a sure thing. Just don't expect lots of licks and nudges from these old (and young) goats.

Capricorn rules the skeleton, knees and teeth. Make sure the food you offer your hoofed or "hoofless" members of this star-studded goat family is full of nutrients, vitamins and minerals (especially calcium and magnesium) to keep their bones and teeth firm and strong. Don't feed your dogs regular meat bones, since the gristle could get caught in their teeth, or worse, in their throat. Buy your Capricorn dogs chewing items that can't splinter or break into small pieces. Give them "chewables" that will really work at keeping their teeth and gums clean and healthy. Since Capricorn animals won't necessarily be the most active ones in your household, make a special effort to see to it that they get plenty of exercise to keep their bones (in particular) in good condition. Be sure not to feed salty items to your Capricorn pet, as a preventive measure against arthritis. Some animals—such as rabbits—do require additional salt in their diet (from a salt lick), so it should not be eliminated in these cases, no matter what their sign is.

Expect your Capricorn dog, bird, rabbit, or even goat, to live to a ripe old age. Capricorn is actually ruled by Father Time (the planet Saturn), and members born under this sign are known to live longer than anyone else. (Guess where the term "old goat" comes from!) You may find that, as your Capricorn pet ages, it seems to get younger. As a puppy, kitten or pony, he or she may seem more typically "Capricornian" (old and rigid) than later on in life—say after the age of five. They may start out somewhat slow and stodgy, often depressed or uninterested in almost everything; then, with time, the Capricornian influence seems to give way to a spry, upbeat, happy animal. This is one sign in which there is a dramatic change in temperament with time.

Even though your Capricorn pet might not be the most animated one of the pack (at least during its early years), you can rest assured that it will prove to be a steadfast, obedient and trusted pal—for a very long time.

Your AQUARIUS Pet
(January 20–February 18)

If you've ever wondered what a real "live wire" pet would be like, get yourself an Aquarius! And I don't mean "live wire" just figuratively, either. These creatures really do like wires! Aquarius has to do with anything electric—anything having to do with wires; so anyone born under its influence is bound to be quite "electric:" very erratic in their actions, and sometimes even quite spacey. People who are Aquarians are naturals when it comes to fixing any wire apparatus; or they just like being around anything with wires. Like really does attract like. The same actually goes for animals. But rather than being able to fix an appliance, your pet guinea pig, cat or ferret might be extraordinarily wired—all the time! I once knew an Aquarius cat who felt most comfortable lying, stretched out, on piles of wires. (Its owner just happened to be an Aquarius also, and, well, that explains all the wires in the house!)

Now, back to the other meaning of "live wire." Your Aquarius pet will probably be anything but calm and easy to manage. Unless you are a little "off the wall" yourself, you'll probably have a challenging time trying to deal with your "live wire." I did have a live, wire-haired terrier, who happened to be an Aquarius. As wonderful as that dog was, it was no picnic; it was more like experiencing a non-stop rollercoaster ride!

The Aquarius energy will make your pet somewhat frenetic—you know, frenzied! It's as if the electrical impulses in their brains keep short-circuiting. The animal, as benevolent as Aquarius tends to be, isn't deliberately uncontrollable, of course. It's just the influence of Aquarius working through it. (Although humans who are born as Aquarians are subject to the same or similar influences, they take this type of "otherworldly" way of being and integrate it in a positive way, creating avant garde, surrealistic or fantastical works of art, either in music, painting, architecture, design or the media.)

It's hard for Aquarius animals to move in any one direction. They seem to move in many directions—all at once! It will be difficult for your Aquarian pet to focus on much of anything (including you), so other than an occasional quick lick or erratic nudging or jumping when they see you, don't expect a lot of attention from this one. Even so, like almost everyone, your Aquarian animal companion could use as much affection as you can muster, for maybe ten seconds, until they short-circuit again, and throw themselves in some other direction.

Aquarius pets are, unfortunately, not the easiest to control or keep track of. If you do have one, make sure there is no way for them to get out of your house or apartment. If there is a way out, they'll find it, and they'll go! They'll probably be back, but in their own time, by their own rules—if they happen to remember the way! The one word that best characterizes Aquarius is independence. If these critters aren't free to do what they darned well please, they'll let you know in no time and in no uncertain terms. Of all the signs of the zodiac, including Sagittarius, Aquarius needs to be free more than any other. When they roam, they may go far. Owner, beware.

As wonderful as your crazy Aquarian animal may be, don't expect much in the way of cuddly affection. We can leave that to the Cancerians and the Leos. A dog born under Aquarius is more independent than any cat you'll ever know (unless the cat is Aquarius). The Aquarian beast is exceedingly friendly to everyone, and yet to no one in particular. They love everyone peripherally—including you! They just like a lot of excitement; even when there isn't any, they'll somehow think (or hope) that something fun is going on, even if they have to act excited—or crazy—all by themselves! At a party, they'll forget you're even there, and happily greet everyone...in a friendly, detached, Aquarian way. Then they'll go find something else to do, for five seconds or less.

Expect even the mellowest of the Aquarian pets to be hyperactive, paranoid, neurotic, disobedient, and not well-disciplined; couple all that with a very short attention span. Here is a perfect example of an animal that moves a lot, but does not necessarily go anywhere.

Aquarius rules the circulation, shins and ankles. Provide an environment for you Aquarian pet which is as soothing to its psyche as possible. Play soft, pleasant music, burn incense, keep the lights low, if possible; that is, keep the electricity at a bare minimum. Try to be around your Aquarian pets as much as possible; the more alone they are, the more mischievous, paranoid and depressed they may become, which, in turn, leads to greater neurosis.

Make sure this animal has plenty of room in which to move, and that it can't get into anything where it can get hurt, especially in the shins and ankles. Because they are so often disoriented, make sure the animal is well acquainted with its surroundings, and try to familiarize it with your neighborhood. It would not be a bad idea to put an identification tag on your pet.

Despite the "short-circuiting" that often afflicts Aquarian pets, they are, nevertheless, very good-natured, not abrasive or aggressive, and make every effort to please you, even though their efforts usually don't take them very far.

Your PISCES Pet
(February 19–March 20)

Have you ever looked at a
dog's eyes, and simply
melted from the goodness
that was expressed by those pools of love? Those
are Pisces eyes. Those are the eyes that we talk
about when we refer to the old adage: "The eyes are
the mirror of the soul." Of course dogs have a soul.
How can we deny it when we can see it—just by
looking at those soulful eyes. Clearly, with some
species of animals (such as rodents or reptiles), it's
difficult to perceive such inner beauty from a

physical standpoint; but that doesn't mean the Pisces energy isn't working through the animal; you just might not see it in the eyes. No matter what species you have, if the animal is a Pisces, it will demonstrate the characteristically benevolent attributes that are typical of that sign.

Pisces is the sign of service—not so much dutiful service as sacrificial service; it is the kind of service that is completely unconditional and carried out for the sole purpose of aiding someone in need.

The dogs that I most often see with those soulful eyes are the seeing eye dogs. It certainly can't be the case that all Seeing Eye dogs are Pisces; but I wouldn't be surprised if there was a strong Piscean influence at work when these dogs were born.

None of this necessarily means that a Pisces animal's only purpose in life is to provide some sort of sacrificial service to its owner. But, among all twelve signs of the zodiac, Pisces seems to be the most evolved to manage such a destiny.

If you have a Pisces pet, he or she is very gentle, "soft-spoken," tenderly affectionate and quite fragile. Their physical and emotional make-ups are not known to be the strongest; they tend to be sensitive to upsets in the home (like emotional outbursts) as well as to ailments in their furry, hairy, feathery or scaly bodies.

A salient trait in your Pisces pet is that it is extraordinarily intuitive...psychic! You may be bewildered by the sensitivity of the animal, a sensitivity that you could swear was otherworldly. Your Pisces pet will be very tuned in to you. No doubt about it: when there is a bond between anyone and a Pisces, there are going to be some very awesome experiences in that relationship. This applies even more to animals since they are not blocked by the concerns of materialism; they are infinitely more in tune and "in sync" with the ways of the Universe than most humans.

Your Pisces pet may do things or even express things to you in ways that will boggle your mind. Perhaps they already have, and you thought there was something eerie (not "eary") about your rabbit or iguana. Pisces pets have a way of communicating with their human companions in uncanny ways—in ways that most people either wouldn't understand or would simply pooh-pooh. This psychic connection is a wonderful experience if you're fortunate enough to have a pet who was born under the sign of the fish.

I had the wonderful and moving experience of owning a Pisces rabbit. Henry didn't know he was a rabbit. He thought he was my alter ego; at times I thought so, too. The psychic connection that I experienced with Henry was profound and lasted as long as he did.

The health of your Pisces pet may not be all that robust. Remember, these creatures tend to be quite fragile. After all, in order to connect with a "higher dimension," they'd have to be more etheric, and not as strong physically.

Treat your Piscean pet with as much tenderness as you can. They truly live just for you, so show them how much you appreciate them. Make sure that air temperatures around them are not extreme—either too hot or too cold. Feeding them a lighter diet is actually better than a lot of heavy foods—no matter what the species is. If it is an animal which must eat large quantities of food, make sure the food is highly nutritious, but not taxing on their delicate systems.

Pisces rules the feet. If your pet has no feet, you don't need to read on. Otherwise keep those paws, claws, hooves and feet well-manicured, clean, trimmed and healthy. Check them periodically for burrs or other little annoyances that can get imbedded in those soulful feet. These problems may become more serious if not tended to right away. Your Pisces pet will be more vulnerable in that area of the body since it is their Achilles heel.

A relationship with an animal companion that is a Pisces can be a very rewarding one. There will be bonding on a level that can not be explained; but you won't need to explain anything. You'll both—somehow—just understand.

Owner and Pet Compatibility

ALTHOUGH IT'S HELPFUL to know an animal's astrological sign, it's more useful when you can see how well its basic personality traits blend with yours, as well as with your lifestyle. If, for example, you have a Cancer dog who likes to cuddle up at home, and you're an adventurous Sagittarian who wants a pet that will accompany you on hikes in the Sierras, and who's not all that demonstrative, you may run into a problem. But rather than get frustrated with your pet, at least you'll understand the motivating forces behind the inharmonious blend of energies.

The reverse can also be true: if you and your pet get along splendidly, astrology will show you why and how that has come to be. If you're thinking about getting a pet, it would help tremendously to know what sign he or she was born under. In that

way, you could get an animal that would be most suited to your own astrological sign, and avoid any regrets or frustration after the fact. Pet stores and breeders often know the birth dates of the animals they sell. If you get your pet by other means, all you need to do is read up on the various astrological signs and go through the check lists in the preceding sections of this book.

The following section pairs you up with your pet and allows you to see why you and your pet do or don't get along so well. If you're contemplating getting a pet, again, checking the compatibility ratings is always better before the fact. To find out how well you and your pet "click," look up your sign first at the beginning of each section; then find your pet's sign. The number of "dog bone" symbols (🦴) after each description of astrological pairs rates the strength of your relationship with your pet. One bone indicates a relationship that doesn't promise a lot. Two bones is a "mediocre" to "good" relationship. Three bones will have you and your pet singing duets, frolicking in the grass, cuddling up in front of the TV, or galloping off into the sunset together. In other words, with three doggie bones, you've met your animal soul mate.

If I'm an ARIES...
and My Pet Is:

ARIES: Establish from the very beginning that YOU are the boss; otherwise the two of you will be sure to "lock horns" from time to time. Aries is used to being "numero uno"; just make sure you're the only one running the show. If you don't, your Aries pet may run amuck, and not obey you, thinking the whole time that he (or she) is the boss! Other than that, your two energies should blend well; you will enjoy traipsing through the wilderness together, throwing the Frisbee or going for long runs on the beach (assuming your pet is so equipped!). A healthy relationship.

TAURUS: You might have a bit too much go power for your Taurus animal companion. Aries has lots of energy; your Taurus pet has energy too, but he or she would rather conserve it, staying closer to home, while you're off seeking some new adventure. Your free-spiritedness may clash with Taurus, especially when the latter gets real bull-headed, won't heed a thing you say, and will do exactly what he or she prefers to do. ⌐⌐

GEMINI: This is a good combination for pet and master. The energy between the two of you runs on "high," and there is a strong, natural bonding. Your Gemini pet will be eager to accompany you on any venture you want to share with him or her, especially if it involves the outdoors or learning new tricks. ⌐⌐ ⌐⌐ ⌐⌐

CANCER: Hopefully, if you happen to have a Cancer pet, he or she won't be too soggy for your fiery Aries temperament. You want to run through the park, but Spot would rather cuddle up and listen to Beethoven. Your Cancer pet may also require a lot more affection than you can muster. 🦴

LEO: This is a great combination. The fire element in both your signs allows for a wonderful interaction between you and your pet—especially when the two of you are engaging in some kind of physical activity. Just remember that *you* are the boss; Leo pets sometimes forget that they can't all be King. 🦴🦴🦴

VIRGO: You may not have the patience required to deal effectively with a Virgo pet. If you have a rabbit or other animal that usually stays in a cage, you probably won't have a problem since Virgo doesn't mind (too much) being alone...and neither do you! But if it's companionship you want with your Virgo pet, the ram and the Virgin don't always make the greatest pair. Aries is very carefree and active, while Virgo is more sedate and mental. While you'd rather be out chasing butterflies, your Virgo cat or dog would probably rather be at home tidying up the litter box or their living quarters. Not the neatest pairing. ⌇⊃

LIBRA: You and your Libra pet can experience a wonderful relationship; this combination allows for much openness and bonding because you are both basically free spirits. Your Libra pet may be a bit demanding of your time, since Libra is a very social animal; but because they don't stomp on your emotional coolness, and prefer to just have you "around," you probably won't feel hampered. A relatively good combination. 🦴 🦴

SCORPIO: This is a somewhat unlikely blend of energies. Being an often capricious type, you may find your Scorpio pet to be a bit too heavy for you. Scorpio tends to like to stay behind the scenes, getting behind the sofa, or hiding out in a closet. Aries likes to get right out in the open, and take the tiger by the tail. Your Scorpio pet couldn't be bothered with such trivialities. he or she would rather be scheming how to get full access to food, how to nab your pet rat, or how to stay out of sight the next time you decide to set out on a new venture. Not your type. 🦴

SAGITTARIUS: Here's probably the best buddy an Aries could have. Whatever you want to do, Sag will be right there with you (at a healthy distance). Sagittarius is a mutable sign, so your pet born under this sign will happily go along with anything you like—and will be doubly happy if it involves a lot of physical activity. 🦴🦴🦴

CAPRICORN: Your Capricorn pet might not be as energetic as you would like. In actuality, Capricorns have plenty of energy; but, like Taurus, it's stored energy, so your pet born under this sign may not burn out as quickly as you. Your pet may not move as fast as your Aries temperament may like, but, like a certain pink rabbit that runs on a well-known battery, they "keep going and going and going." 🦴 🦴

AQUARIUS: You should get along rather well with your Aquarius pet. Though you both have a lot of energy, your Aquarius pet runs mostly on nervous energy, which, at one point, may drive even you a little crazy. You may have to keep watch on your pet to make sure he or she is in "sync" with you, especially if you go out for a trot, a walk or a swim. 🦴 🦴

PISCES: If you're looking for excitement, spontaneity and exuberance in your pet, being an Aries, you may be disappointed if your pet is a Pisces. Your Pisces pet will be more fragile and sensitive than what you need to keep your Aries fiery nature burning. As a companion, Pisces may be too soft for your often brusque way, and your pet will probably not get the tenderness that it needs in return. This is not the greatest combination.

If I'm a TAURUS...

and My Pet Is:

ARIES: You're either too slow for your pet, or your pet's too active for your taste. Either way, you will admire your pet's spunk and vivaciousness, and sometimes wish you had as much "get-up-and-go" as he or she does. If anything, your pet will spur you on to get moving, whether it's to go for a run (maybe a slow run in your case), to climb a rock, or simply to go outside and soak up some sunshine. (Aries is a fire sign, and does enjoy the sun.) Even though you may not be up to the ways of your Aries animal companion, you will be tolerant and accepting of his or her extraordinary vitality. 🦴🦴

TAURUS: Neither one of you may want to go out and do much of anything. Both of you may prefer to just stay at home, watch TV...and eat! With humans, this combination isn't necessarily all that great: they both may end up in the same rut and eventually get bored with each other. Taurus usually likes to stay put. With the animal–human combination, you'll have your "buddy" right next to you, all the time, keeping you company while you putter around the house. No complaints, no agitation, just down-home comfort. 🦴🦴🦴

GEMINI: This could be interesting—and nerve-wracking at the same time! Since Gemini runs on a lot of nervous energy, and Taurus tends to be more grounded, your Gemini pet may give you a run for your money. Your pet will, more than likely, expect to be constantly entertained, either by a variety of toys, learning new tricks...or you! But since you'd probably rather stay put, you may sometimes feel a bit frazzled by your Gemini pet—especially if it is a dog, a bird or a monkey. 🦴

CANCER: Here you have a cozy combination. You're both the "stay-at-home" types and you're both pretty tactile, so you probably won't mind if Rover stays permanently attached to your leg (something he wouldn't mind at all). There may be times, however, when your Cancer pet requires a lot more affection than your somewhat reserved Taurean nature can muster. He or she may whine, yelp, cry, groan, whimper or grunt just enough to make you lose your patience—something you don't do very often. You'll both be happy staying at home, for the most part, and you'll also enjoy eating together—a favorite pastime for both of you! (Just remember not to overindulge your Cancer pet—especially dogs; Cancer rules the stomach, so this part of the body is particularly sensitive and vulnerable to problems in Cancer natives.)

LEO: Both you and your Leo pet are fixed signs which means that you both have the tendency to be set in your ways; and your ways may be very different at that! Leo, being a fire sign, will be set on being active; so your pet will often seek different forms of high-energy activity. Whether you're up to it or not, your pet may use his Leonine ways to get you to do what he wants. Don't forget, we're dealing with Leo the Lion—the King! You may actually find your Leo pet to be quite dazzling in the way he or she tries to run the show. But if you're true to your Taurean nature, you'll be patient with your Leo companion and admire the beauty of his ways. You both like luxury, so if you don't mind your Leo pet getting up on your silk chaise lounge, he won't mind your getting on his velvet armchair—his throne! 🦴 🦴

VIRGO: Here's a likely pair. You like being catered to, and your Virgo pet likes taking care of you. What more could you ask for? Even if your pet's services are "limited," due to the type of animal it is, you will still sense that there is a deep caring that your pet feels for you. You like things pretty, Virgo likes things neat. So, you won't have to worry about your Virgo pet messing up your pretty house...or his or her house, either, for that matter! Things will run smoothly between you and your Virgo pet. Your pet will comply with all your wishes, and will always be devoted and constant. Your energies, likes, and dislikes are parallel. ⌧ ⌧ ⌧

LIBRA: If your pet is a Libra, your Taurean nature will value its sense of serenity and calm. Although your Libran pet is very intelligent, it's airy nature does not render it spacy or out of control, such as pets born under the other air signs of Gemini and Aquarius; instead, your pet will be "quietly alert" and ready for any interaction you propose. And not being all that physically active, you will enjoy your Libra pet's calmness, and you will find its mental acuteness very refreshing. ⌧ ⌧

SCORPIO: This relationship between you and your pet should be a very pleasant one. Neither one of you is apt to want to go romping through the woods or blazing trails—at least not very often or for any length of time. You're both relatively affectionate and will have very strong feelings for each other. (You'll sense this easily from your Scorpio pet.) Even though your emotions run deep, you and your Scorpio pet both tend to control your emotions; so you probably won't get a lot of outbursts or uncontrollable displays of emotion from your Scorpio pet as you would from an Aries or a Cancer pet. This is just fine with you since your temperament is basically the same. 🦴🦴🦴

SAGITTARIUS: A Taurus owner of a Sagittarian pet is somewhat of an incongruous combination, similar to the relationship you would have with an Aries pet. You'll probably be in awe of your pet's physical agility, strength and energy, even though it may tire you out just watching him or her. Being under the influence of a mutable sign, your Sagittarian pet will be quite adaptable; thus, even if it would rather not do a particular activity (like wait in the car for you for half an hour), it will usually go along with the plan. (If you make this animal wait any longer, your car may not be in the greatest shape when you return. Sagittarians can't control their bountiful energy for too long.) You may find that a hyperactive Sagittarius pet is more than your sedate temperament can handle. But you will cherish his or her noble ways, and your pet, in turn, will feel safe and secure with your solid, kindly manner. 🦴 🦴

CAPRICORN: You and your Capricornian pet will get along so famously that you will sometimes wonder if he or she was heaven-sent. You are both Earth signs, so you're bound to hit it off right from the start, just because of that. Temperamentally, you and your Capricorn goat, parrot, German Shepherd, mutt, or any other species are very similar; you don't emote a lot and you don't get angry too easily, either. In fact, you may get more than you'd like of your own medicine: Capricorn can be very cold, so don't expect much affection from this pet. Your Capricorn pet will not expect much (if any) from you, either. ⌑⌑⌑

AQUARIUS: If there's one pet that might push a Taurus owner over the edge, this one is it. Your Taurean endurance may actually run out if you have an Aquarius pet—especially one that doesn't live in a cage. If you were less earthy and grounded (like a

Gemini or an Aries), you'd probably think your beloved Aquarian Fox Terrier, iguana or Himalayan cat was "cute" with its erratic tendencies. But your Taurean nature does not take well to energy that is not channeled—anywhere. You'd like an animal that responds to you—somehow. You'd like an animal that even knows you're around. Not the greatest match. 🦴

PISCES: Here's another good pal for the Taurus pet owner. Gentle, quiet, undemanding and attentive; just the way you like it. Your Pisces pet will be another good candidate for an occasional swim in the pool or walk on the beach, if you're up to it. This relationship should be smooth, pleasant and totally to your liking. Your Pisces pet will be just the balm you need after a hectic day. You'll love this one. 🦴🦴🦴

If I'm a GEMINI...

and My Pet Is:

ARIES: Here's a great combination. You'll have a lot of fun with your Aries pet. After all, FUN is what you both seek. Whatever you're up to, be sure to let your Aries animal companion in on it, too...as long as it's not too mental. Being more physical than mental, the Aries idea of "fun" is a hike in the mountains or a run on the beach in the summer. You, Gemini, can get into that, too, but you're also highly active mentally. Don't forget about

Felix when you're on one of your frivolous mental journeys. 🦴 🦴 🦴

TAURUS: You may expect more from your Taurus pet than he can—or chooses to—deliver. You may want to teach Tweedle Dee a myriad of tricks, but chances are you won't budge her. Taurus is very set, and Gemini is very flexible. You're both pretty good-natured, so one of you will eventually give in—and it will probably be you. 🦴

GEMINI: You and your Gemini pet will have a ball together, constantly getting into all kinds of mischief. You'll teach him some tricks, and he may teach you a few! You'll be mentally and physically "in sync," and each of you will be a great "energizer" for the other. Even though you probably look very different, you and your Gemini pet will be similar in every other way. Your pet will likely even have a sense of humor (many animals do, especially if they are Geminis). Each of you will feed off the other and life will be a lot of fun. 🦴 🦴 🦴

CANCER: You may not have the patience—or the time—for your Cancer pet's emotional needs. You're not big on affection, but Cancer is. Your Cancer pet would love it if you would caress him or her forever; but your idea of "forever" is about ten seconds. The kind of attention you'd be willing to give a Cancerian animal is not in keeping with the needs of an animal born under the influence of the moon. You also may not have the patience for this pet's mood swings. Unless there's someone else in your household who can "mother" your Cancer pet, either try to muster a little more affection than you're used to giving, or, if possible, get a pet that's more in keeping with your temperament, like a Sagittarian or an Aquarian. 🦴

LEO: You and your Leo pet should get along great, as long as you defer to your pet (or at least make him or her think that's what you're doing). Fire (Leo) and air (Gemini) always work—and play— well together. You both have plenty of energy and stamina. You're both bound to be quite playful together, with neither one rubbing the other the wrong way. Just don't agitate your Leo buddy; they have no problem letting you know when you're out of line: you could get bitten, whacked or pecked if you don't live up to Leo's high standards of "respect." 🦴 🦴 🦴

VIRGO: You will communicate famously with your Virgo pet. He or she will understand and quickly respond to your requests and dutifully carry them out. At times, though, you may actually come to annoy this demure creature, who, for the most part, would like to be left alone, rather than be incessantly needled by a mischievous Gemini. For the most part, though, your temperaments are relatively well suited to each other. 🦴 🦴

LIBRA: You should have no problems whatsoever with your Libra pet. You and your pet resonate to the same music. You are both more mental than physical, and yet, you'll get no resistance from Libra when you want to go for a skip around the block—especially if there are other "creatures" for Libra to socialize with out there. The two of you will feel a strong camaraderie, both mentally as well as physically. The energies flow smoothly and there should rarely, if ever, be any snags in your relationship. ⊂⊃ ⊂⊃ ⊂⊃

SCORPIO: A Scorpio pet with a Gemini owner: interesting—especially since Scorpio likes to be the one to run things—to *control* things. It's good that you're not too demanding; that way there won't be much friction between you and the scorpion. Scorpio does what it wants to do, when it wants to do it, and how it wants to do it, whether it's an animal or a human. Your Scorpio pet may seem too mellow for you, but, in actuality, he or she is right on top of things, quietly checking everything to make sure that all is in order. They are smarter than you may think. They'll see their Gemini "owner" (a misnomer here) as someone who indulges in frivolous and senseless behavior. Your Scorpio pet really has no use for such interaction that involves learning tricks or playing "fetch." They're far too superior to that. Your best bet is to just let them do their thing, and go find yourself another Gemini to play with. 🦴

SAGITTARIUS: Here is your dream companion. If Gemini could magically whip up his perfect animal counterpart, he would ask Genie for a Sagittarius. There's not much else to say other than that you and your Sagittarius pet could easily become best friends. 🦴🦴🦴

CAPRICORN: Probably the one thing that you and your Capricorn pet have in common is that neither of you is all that warm or affectionate. It doesn't mean that you don't have feelings; it's just that you'd rather not expose those feelings. On that note, you and the goat won't lock horns. Capricorn is very determined and unswerving in its desires. Gemini gets bored easily and can quickly change from one interest to another. This is where you and your Capricorn pet might not see eye to eye. This pet of yours could spend hours trying to locate that bone that he or she buried a year ago, and not give up 'til it's found. If it's a Capricorn cat you've got, the search for a particular mouse could last for days. If you've got other items on your agenda that also include your pet, you may have a hard time tearing him away from his very important, self-imposed task. Capricorn is another sign that likes to run things, so don't expect it to be to easy to sway your pet from what it wants to do. ⌒⫘

AQUARIUS: An Aquarius pet could be a lot of fun for you, Gemini. Although Aquarius is "fixed" and you're "mutable," you are still both "air" signs, which means you have similar tendencies, likes and dislikes. Your Aquarius pet, like you, runs principally on nervous energy, so neither one will necessarily tire the other out. Although your Aquarius bird or iguana may not be as focused as you'd like, you still enjoy their fun-loving, friendly way. They also prefer not to get too friendly, so neither one of you will infringe on the other; you'll give each other a fair amount of attention without either one of you expecting much more from the other. The two of you can entertain yourselves—or each other—while maintaining a relatively healthy distance from each other. 🦴 🦴 🦴

PISCES: Your Pisces pet may not be spunky enough for your energetic Gemini nature. Pisces requires a soothing existence, one in which the energy level is low, and the tenderness level is high. Such gaging for Gemini seems to be the reverse. You probably won't get most of what you'd like from your Pisces pet (i.e. spontaneity, vivaciousness and alertness); and your Pisces pet may feel deprived of what it needs as well (i.e. lots of affection, a quiet environment and, most of all....you!).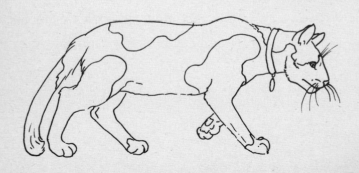

If I'm a CANCER...
and My Pet Is:

ARIES: Here's the probable scenario: your pet always wants to be on the go, and you always want to stay home. If you have an Aries rabbit that's caged, this rabbit will always want to come out; this would be fine with you if the rabbit would just stay still and cuddle a while. Not likely. Rabbit will be all over the place, full of energy and rarin' to go. This applies to most of your other relationships with Aries pets. If it's a horse that you've got, you'd love to groom it all day long; but he (or she) would much rather run around the track a few times. Not a great match.

TAURUS: The same holds true here as for when you are the Taurus and your pet is the Cancer. You're both homebodies, you both like to eat, and neither of you is big on exercise. You're both tender, although you will require more affection than your Taurus pet. Also, the fact that you're a water sign may often give you the urge to be near water or even jump right in. Take your Taurus pet, too. Being an Earth sign, your pet will find the water cool and soothing. A good combo. 🦴🦴🦴

GEMINI: You're going to need a lot more attention from your Gemini pet than you're probably going to get. Gemini is very frivolous—whether it's a human, a dog, a cat or an alien. Gemini doesn't' take things very seriously, and it doesn't require (or give) much affection. So, figure it out: Would a nervous, very active, inattentive Gemini be the ideal pet for an often needy, moody, sedate and affectionate Cancer master? No way. ⊂⊃

CANCER: You and your Cancer pet can cry together, eat together (don't eat too much, though), cuddle together, and you'll both be all the better for it. There's a mutual understanding between you and your pet that not even your own mother can understand (unless she's a Cancer, too). If you're up to it, let your Cancer pet sleep in the same room with you; by all means, never make it sleep outside. You two should get along famously; just be careful that you don't get too attached to each other and forget that there's a bigger world out there, apart from the comforts of home. ⊂⊃ ⊂⊃ ⊂⊃

LEO: This could be a rather good relationship. Both you and your Leo pet are bound to be affectionate with each other. You'll be loving and caring toward your Leo pet. You will be in awe of his or her energy and elegance. Your Leo pet will soak up all the adulation you can send its way; being a Cancer, this should be no problem for you. This relationship could thus be somewhat unbalanced, with you doing most of the giving, and your Leo pet doing most of the self-indulging—not an uncommon thing for Leo to do. 🦴 🦴

VIRGO: The reciprocity between you and your Virgo pet could get out of hand; but it should prove to be healthy for both of you, since you like to nurture, and so does Virgo, but in a more cool, detached manner than you. So you'll provide most of the affection, and your Virgo pet will dutifully tend to your needs, be there when you need him or her, and always be trustworthy and loyal. Virgo, like you, also enjoys the comforts of home. You and your Virgo pet should be quite compatible, though the latter may tone down any potential emotionality. ⬭⬭

LIBRA: Since your Libra pet enjoys the comforts of home as well as companionship, and so do you, the two of you should have a relatively good relationship. Your Libran companion, however, enjoys "togetherness" in a more distanced manner than that which might suit you. Your pet likes to know that you are "around." You'd like to have more "personal" contact with your pet. There will have to be a compromise, but your Libra pet will probably win. They're just not all that affectionate. So call your mother when you need a shoulder to cry on, Cancer. ⊂⊃ ⊂⊃

SCORPIO: Both you and your Scorpio pet were born (or hatched) under water signs, so you'll both be very emotional and feeling. Your Scorpio pet, however, will not be as demonstrative as you, even though the deep feelings and unwavering devotion will be there; you just won't always see it. You'll tend to *feel* it more than anything. Scorpio has a keen sense of perception—like extrasensory perception; so your Scorpio pet will often sense your needs or wishes, and do whatever is in his or her power to help you out. Pay close attention to how your Scorpio pet relates to you. You may find this animal to be uncanny—especially when relating to *you*. A good relationship. ⊂⊃ ⊂⊃ ⊂⊃

SAGITTARIUS: A Sagittarius animal may not be the perfect pet for you, Cancer. Whatever species you have, as long as it's a Sagittarian, it will require a lot of physical activity. It's not too likely that you'll be able to keep up with this pet in the exercise department. Besides that, your Sagittarius pet is not going to be around, at any point, long enough for you two to bond on an emotional level. Emotional bonding is very important to you; but, woe is you, your Sagittarian pet would just as soon leave all that "mushy stuff" by the wayside and go on an adventure (like flying around the block, going mouse-hunting, or climbing a mountain!). ⌇

CAPRICORN: Interestingly, Cancer and Capricorn get along quite well, considering the fact that you are a warm, affectionate soul, and Capricorn is just the opposite. But, astrologically speaking, the energies between Cancer and Capricorn—whatever the species—seem to blend quite nicely. So, even though your Capricorn dog or horse may seem distant, you'll feel somehow connected and definitely in tune with them. Opposites really do attract!

AQUARIUS: You'll, at times, wonder what it was that ever possessed you to get your Aquarian pet in the first place. (If you're still debating and haven't obtained it yet, don't!) He or she is everything that goes against your grain. You won't be happy, and neither will your pet.

PISCES: You two should hit it off from the start, even though your relationship with your Pisces pet won't be anything flamboyant. It will be more like a glass of warm milk: soothing, pleasant and just plain nice. Your Pisces cat or dog will find comfort in your gentle caresses, and you will find comfort in the peaceable, mystical qualities of your Pisces pet. The two of you will enjoy quiet times together. 🦴 🦴 🦴

If I'm a LEO...
and My Pet Is:

ARIES: Your energy levels should be comparable, except your batteries might be better charged than those of your Aries dog or horse. There's no doubt about who will be in charge: you will. Your Aries pet may try to take over the reins, but Aries is no match for Leo when it comes to running the show. Let your pet know early on "who's the boss," and you should rarely, if ever, have any run-ins. Your Aries pet will "just know" not to challenge his or her Leo master, and will know to live up to what Leo—that's you—expects most in life: RESPECT. You'll get respect from Aries; although, at times, your Aries pet's temper may get the better of him or her. (They are very hot-headed.) All in all, you and your Aries pet should enjoy life together, whether traveling, playing in the back yard, or watching the playoffs on TV. 🦴 🦴 🦴

TAURUS: You probably won't encounter any problems with your Taurean pet. For the most part, she will defer to your wishes—except when she doesn't want to. The only real downfall of Taurus is that they are extremely stubborn. This doesn't go over that well with Leo, who's also stubborn, and even more determined than Taurus to get her way. So, you may need to remind your little Taurean chickadee, dog or cat who the boss is. You may get through to them and you may not. But you'll love your Taurus pet no matter what; they're just so good. They won't get in your way, they won't beg (except maybe for food), you don't have to keep them busy all the time, and, overall, they make a quiet companion for Leo. 🦴 🦴

GEMINI: Gemini is a good choice as a pet for a Leo type like yourself. Your Gemini pet will be flexible and go along with anything you suggest—just the way you like it! You'll enjoy their yielding ways as well as their constant sense of fun and frivolity. Your Gemini pet will share your enthusiasm for adventure and will serve as a great companion in any variety of activities that you may choose to do. 🦴 🦴 🦴

CANCER: You may find that your Cancer pet is a bit too wimpy for your taste and purposes. You're an adventurer, full of energy and zest for life. Your Cancer pet would rather stay at home, taking care of you—or have you taking care of him! Although you are big-hearted and can appreciate the sensitive nature of your Cancer dog, bird or ferret, it's not in your make-up to sit at home, catering to a needy pet; after all, *you* are the one who expects to be catered to. You'd like it if your Cancerian pet would just go along with the program, and stop being so "childish." Cancer would willingly do what you'd like, as long as it didn't involve such strenuous activity. They'd rather stay at home.

LEO: This could go one of two ways: well or badly. It all depends on how dogmatic you both are. If you both want your way, if neither of you gives in, your relationship with your Leo pet won't go so well. You do have one advantage, however: you're human. A human Leo has a lot more clout than an animal who is a Leo; you just have to convince the animal of that; it may not be so easy. If you do end up "having it out" with your Leo pet, if he simply won't bend to your ways, you may have to be very strong and not let the animal pull any punches. Once your Leo pet knows that he really can't be the boss, he may have a hard time going against his true nature at first; but, with time, and with your love and strength, the animal will come to respect you, and, more importantly, obey you. On the other hand, Leo can be so noble as to 'simply know' that you're his master, and that will be enough for him. ⊂⊃ ⊂⊃

VIRGO: Even though you are "fire" and your Virgo pet is "earth," when human and animal experience a relationship together, this combination isn't all that negative. You won't have to let Virgo know that you're in charge. He or she already knows it. They like to be subservient, so a Leo master sits well with your Virgo pet—at least in that vein. Your Virgo pet may or may not have a lot of energy; they tend to have more stamina than energy. So, if you decided to go on a nice, long walk, your Virgo pet might like that. But a long, arduous triathlon probably wouldn't go over too well with this animal. Your Virgo pet will obey you right from the get-go, and will always make an effort to please you. ⊂⊃ ⊂⊃

LIBRA: Both you and your Libra pet need a family, even if it's just the two of you that make up that family. You both need companionship, and since air (Libra) and fire (Leo) work well together, your relationship with your Libra pet should be very rewarding. Your pet will be happy to have you lead as long as you don't mind waiting while he or she stops to smell the roses. 🦴 🦴 🦴

SCORPIO: This should be interesting. You both like to lead, you're both relentless, you're both strong as nails, and, even though *you* are the human, your Scorpio pet has incredible ways of manipulating you or a situation to get things his or her own way. Say you want your Scorpio pet to try some new food. You take his old food away—the food he likes. You put the new food out, expecting that eventually he will eat it. Guess what. If your pet's a Scorpio, it would rather die than give in to something it doesn't want to do. He won't eat the new food. So you start to worry. That's exactly what he wants you to do. So you give him back his old food. Who won? You've met your match with this one, Leo. 🦴

SAGITTARIUS: You'll get along great with any Sagittarian pet you may have. First and foremost, you get to be the boss. Then, they like to have fun, just like you do. They've also got as much energy as you do, and are very pliable, so they'll like anything you suggest. If you've got a Sagittarian iguana or rabbit, you won't mind chasing it all over the back yard while it tries to get away; you'll just see it as an exciting challenge, something Leos can't live without. If you've got a dog, you'll be pals for life, and you'll experience a very healthy camaraderie, seldom had among humans. It's the kind of relationship where you say "Jump," and your pet says "How high?" 🦴 🦴 🦴

CAPRICORN: There can only be one general, one captain, one master. And you'd better let your

Capricorn dog, cat, bird or goat know from the start that it's you! A Capricorn pet can be a nice pet to have as long as it's not always bent on having its own way. Unlike you, your pet is cold and aloof, so you're already off to a bad start. This creature is masterful in getting you to do what he or she wants! My Capricorn dog has me jumping hoops incessantly...much more than my Leo dog. If she (the Capricorn) wants water, she'll throw the dish around until it either breaks or I get her the water. Five minutes later, she decides she wants to "go out." The door either gets totally destroyed or I get up to let her out. Your Capricorn pet, if true to its nature, will be relentless until it gets what it wants. It has little style, and virtually no grace. All it ever has is a purpose, a goal—and it's usually at your expense! 🦴

AQUARIUS: An Aquarius pet will be like a breath of fresh air for you, Leo, especially after you've spent some time with your Capricorn pet. (If you're lucky, that won't be the case.) You'll like the spontaneity of your Aquarian cat, pig or bird, but at times you may feel that he or she is a bit detached and "spacey"; you may not feel all that connected even though you sense that there is some strong bond that keeps the two of you best friends. ⬭ ⬭ ⬭

PISCES: Leo, you may tend to be a bit too brusque for your fragile Pisces pet. Remember, not everyone is strong, powerful and energetic like you. Humble, retiring Pisces may come out of its hiding place to worship its master (that's you), but it probably won't have the spunk and vitality that you wish it did to indulge you in your bombastic life. No, no;

your Pisces pet needs tranquillity and gentleness, the quiet life. Maybe a little walk or a gentle swim from time to time. So don't let that healthy (big) ego of yours get in the way and force these gentle creatures into doing things that are not in keeping with their frail Piscean nature.

If I'm a VIRGO...

and My Pet Is:

ARIES: You're just too much of a fuddy-duddy to have any kind of an Aries around the house—especially when it's an animal! Unless your Aries pet is a sloth, you would do better with almost any other sign (Sagittarius and Aquarius excepted). You like things "under control"; your Aries pet is definitely not that! You're relatively placid, and your Aries pet is very active. Although you enjoy engaging in various interesting activities and your energy level is on the high side, your temperament does not harmonize with the fiery, often uncontrollable nature of Aries the ram. You'd like a pet you could have inside with you, who would calmly listen to your complaints and watch your favorite TV shows with you. Aries could never do that; your Aries pet would want to be outside all the time—with you, throwing the Frisbee for six hours. Not the greatest match.

TAURUS: You'll like your Taurus pet. Like you, he's even-tempered, well-behaved and likes to ride in the car (so he probably won't throw up!). You'll probably be the one to give in when your Taurus pet is having one of his "stubborn" sessions; but you're understanding enough to realize that it's just an occasional thing and that, for the most part, your Taurean pet and you make a great team.

GEMINI: Even though your temperaments are not perfectly matched, you and your Gemini pet may share some scintillating moments. You'll be flexible enough to indulge Gemini in short, sweet games or romps. However, your Gemini pet may not have the patience to sit around watching you knit or straighten up the house. You like to teach and your Gemini pet likes to learn; so that's probably where you two could connect the most. The more things you teach your Gemini bird, iguana or dog (in short doses), the happier you both will be and the healthier your relationship will be. If you don't have this type of interaction, you both may wind up driving each other crazy. 🦴 🦴

CANCER: Cancer and Virgo do well together, even when one's an animal and the other is a human. You and your Cancer pet will enjoy being together in the comforts of home; be sure to let your Cancer pet stay inside—near you—as much as possible. One of the main things that Virgo rules is (small) animals. Therefore, you will probably enjoy taking care of your Cancer pet (even if it's a big one); and your Cancer pet will lap up as much care as you can give him or her. You'll both feel rewarded by each other's companionship. 🦴 🦴 🦴

LEO: Virgo has to put her (or his) softer Virgoan ways on the back burner when dealing with your Leo pet. This animal can be a wonderful, devoted friend to you, but you'd better make sure early on that this same animal doesn't try to pull rank on you (Leo is King, remember). Letting Leo know that someone else is the boss can often be a hard thing for Leos to take; but, being as noble as they are, your Leo pet will give in with time. Don't expect a total metamorphosis, however; the Leo energy will never cease to have some influence on your pet; he or she may, at times, try to get the upper hand (I'm sure you've already seen it), but, bear in mind that this is just in keeping with the nature of things. Your pet will sense your genuine caring for it, and will usually obey you. The only down side between you and your Leo pet may be that he or she has more energy than you can handle. Not a bad combination.

VIRGO: Virgo with Virgo doesn't usually fair well when both are humans; but with human and animal, the compatibility rate rises substantially. You and your Virgo pet have a lot in common: you both like to keep to yourselves, even though you'll often seek out each other's company; you'll be close, but you won't get in each other's way. Your pet won't mess up your house (or his or hers) and your levels of energy will be about on par, as well. For you, Virgo, your Virgo pet won't be difficult to train, to talk to, to understand, to take care of...or to love. ▱ ▱ ▱

LIBRA: You both like to keep the peace; neither one of you is big on making waves. Your Libra pet will be quite amenable to your ways, even if you may be a bit demanding at times. Libra will just take it in stride, give you a little nudge for reassurance, a little tail-wag to let you know you're still all right in their book, or a little meow to let you know they still love you. Even though you are a mutable sign, Virgo, you're not always that flexible. You may be a bit too finicky or nit-picking with your Libra pet, who isn't all that concerned about details. Give your Libra pet some slack; let him get on the sofa for a change or sit next to you while you eat. Your Libra pet is full of love; let him express it in his way. 🦴 🦴

SCORPIO: You two may sit staring at each other all day, trying to figure each other out. Or, if you're lucky, you'll both rise above all that intrigue and really enjoy each other's company. There's no reason why you and your Scorpio dog, monkey or iguana can't get along well. To some extent, you may even identify with your Scorpio pet: you're pretty quiet, so is your pet; you're very observant, so is your pet; you can be really nasty...so can your Scorpio pet—

big time! So now that you recognize the situation, it's up to you to establish the right relationship with your Scorpio pet. Don't antagonize it, don't challenge it, and don't make it think that you're the boss. At least try to keep things equal. Your aim should be to always keep your Scorpio pet...happy. This could be interesting. 🦴 🦴

SAGITTARIUS: Your Sagittarian pet may prove to be a bit too wild for your taste. You like to direct your energies methodically and quietly. Sagittarius likes to do things gregariously and ubiquitously. You'll want to stay put and get things done, but your Sagittarian pet will probably have a different agenda, the likes of which will more than likely involve some kind of physical activity. It will be hard to keep your Sagittarian cat, dog or horse quiet while you busy yourself with all your Virgo chores. Here's a likely scenario between you and this very energetic animal: he or she wants to go, you want to stay; he or she wants to play, you want to work; he or she will continuously prefer to be active, where you can only take that in short doses. The principle game that will be played in this relationship is "tug-o-war."

CAPRICORN: Your Capricorn pet and you will probably get along quite well. Your temperaments are similar. You'll both enjoy each other's company because you are both mild and can usually remain very content, close to each other, but within your own little worlds. Your Capricorn pet won't find the need to always be around you, or do anything that's contrary to what you're happy doing. Neither of you is all that effusive, but that's all right because neither of you relates very well to emotional displays. You give each other an adequate amount of affection (you probably more than your pet), and you will both accept that as a satisfactory, comfortable interaction. 🦴 🦴 🦴

AQUARIUS: You are much too organized and sedate to put up with the likes of an Aquarius pet for long. This pet will be too much for you to handle: it will often be out of control, not be very responsive to you, and totally throw you off of your stable, Virgoan system of doing things. Not very promising this one. 🦴

PISCES: You will be everything to your Pisces pet that he or she would have ordered for an owner.

Your sensitivity (not often displayed for all to see) will abound toward your Pisces pet; you will sense a link to him that will compel you to pull out all the stops in fully expressing your Virgo nature, to do what Virgos do best: take care of others. Since Virgo rules animals, you'll excel at taking care of your Piscean pet; it will not only seem natural to you, but you will totally enjoy the experience and feel very emotionally rewarded for it. Your Piscean pet will, in turn, lovingly soak up all the care that you show him or her, and will be devoted to you for life. You will both express gentleness and much love to each other. Beautiful. 🦴 🦴 🦴

If I'm a LIBRA...

and My Pet Is:

ARIES: Traditionally this combination works well, but your Aries pet may require a bit more managing than you may be interested in dishing out. Even though your energies won't clash (air and fire), Aries has a lot more energy than Libra— a lot more! You'll have patience with your Aries pet, but you just may choose not to go on twelve walks a day! ⊂≡⊃ ⊂≡⊃

TAURUS: You and your Taurus pet should enjoy a pleasant home life together. Your relationship may not be anything extraordinary, but you will respect each other's space and express enough affection for each other to keep the relationship healthy. Taurus is usually too slow and heavy for air signs (like Gemini and Aquarius); but Libra tends to be more sedate than the other two air signs, and enjoys the simple pleasures of home and companionship— including that of an animal. 🦴 🦴

GEMINI: For humans, Libra and Gemini is a great combination. For a relationship between human and animal, it may be another story. Both you and your Gemini pet were born under "air" signs, which is good for general compatibility. However, you, Libra, will tend to be more sedentary than your Gemini animal companion, who will, more often than not, be very active. Another "however" is that you are both very active mentally. So there should be some sort of common ground on a mental level: you will either be able to communicate mentally, or your pet will enjoy endless tricks that you will tirelessly teach him or her; or you will both simply enjoy some intangible linkage, even though you may not be able to pinpoint what it is. ᘖ ᘖ ᘖ

CANCER: Unless you are an exception to the rule, your Libran nature won't take too kindly to your Cancerian pet's constant need for attention. You enjoy companionship (with anyone) on a somewhat "friendly" level. You try to keep emotions from getting in the way. Your Cancer pet may not see it that way. He or she will expect to be with you all the time; he or she will expect constant care and tenderness from you. If you can not provide those things, you'll have a pet who is not very gratified. You both could do better. ⌐⌐

LEO: Your Leo pet should bring you much enjoyment, admiration and pride. You won't need much inventiveness to keep this creature entertained; they are pretty self-sufficient and literally enjoy just being alive! You'll both enjoy the fresh air and sunshine of the outdoors. (Leo loves the sun and you love the outdoors.) There will always be sparks (good ones) between you and your Leo pet: a high energy level, lots of enthusiasm and good feelings. A keeper. ⌐⌐ ⌐⌐ ⌐⌐

VIRGO: You could get along quite well with your Virgo animal partner. You'll understand each other;

you'll recognize each other's needs, likes and dislikes, and act accordingly. You both like the same amount of physical activity (which isn't a lot), and neither one of you is very emotionally needy. This combination works better this way than with the owner being the Virgo and the pet being Libra. You will probably be more flexible and permissive than a Virgo pet owner would be. You won't need to worry about being a disciplinarian with your Virgo pet, anyway, since they instinctively know how to behave. This should work. ⌒⊃ ⌒⊃

LIBRA: You and your Libra pet will have a jolly old time...all the time. You two will just naturally click, whether it's a bird that you have, a horse, a dog or even an iguana. You'll constantly have lots of fun together, either indulging in laziness, prancing around the garden, or just having a mental tête-a-tête. This one's fun. ⬡ ⬡ ⬡

SCORPIO: You may feel something for your Scorpio pet, but you might be somewhat unsure as to what that "something" is. You probably won't have a lot in common. Your Scorpio dog or cat will prefer to keep to him or herself for the most part, but you usually like some kind of interaction. You like to be "friendly" and companionable; your Scorpio pet couldn't care less about those things. Chances are, you'll want to frolic or just "relate," and chances are even greater that your Scorpio pet will just glare at you with those penetrating eyes, as if to say: "Leave me alone." Good luck. ⬡

SAGITTARIUS: You'll enjoy your Sagittarian pony, pig or Doberman (or any other Sagittarian beast) in spurts. Their high energy level will get you out of your Libran lethargy from time to time, and you'll feel energized—for all of about fifteen minutes; then you'll go back to your book, TV or phone conversation, and feel like you've gotten your exercise for the day. But you forgot Rover. He's still waiting for you to come back and throw the squeaky rubber lamb chop another six hundred times so he can retrieve it another six hundred times. Your Sag pet may wear you out, but you'll love him (or her) just the same. 🦴 🦴

CAPRICORN: If you ever wanted to find a pet as unlike you as possible, you'd find it in a Capricorn. You, Libra, like to enjoy life, play, relax, chat, spend easy time; Capricorn says "no" to all that—even if they're an animal. A Capricorn animal obviously won't be concerned about paying the bills or "getting the job done," like a human Capricorn would. But there is still a coldness, an aloofness, a strong earthiness and heaviness to the Capricorn nature that carries over into the animal world; you, Libra, may not take very well to this. Your Capricorn pet's nature is antithetical to your own, and you may just as soon do without any pet at all if this is the only astrological sign you can find. ⌬

AQUARIUS: Although you may sometimes observe your Aquarian pet and question its sanity, you'll still find it engaging, interesting and strangely attractive to the eye. Your Aquarian dog, cat or rabbit (et al) will constantly capture your attention, either because of its unpredictably erratic behavior or because of some strange quirk that you just can't seem to figure out. But, unlike other astrological signs, you'll be less annoyed by your four-legged, two-legged or "legless" Aquarian; your exchange of energies should, for the most part, be healthy and definitely invigorating. 🦴 🦴 🦴

PISCES: Even though you like companionship, you also like your space. Your Pisces pet may not allow you all the space you require. Being a water sign to boot, this animal may be more than your emotionally cool nature can handle. He or she will need more affection than any other kind of attention. If you're not willing—or simply can't fit that in—find somebody who can. Pisces can't live without it. 🦴

If I'm a SCORPIO...

and My Pet Is:

ARIES: This pet may be too out of control for you. The animal itself isn't necessarily out of control; it's just that it seems that way when paired up with a Scorpio master. You both have lots of energy, but yours is below the surface, and your Aries pet's energy is right out there in the open—in bushels! If you are true to your Scorpio nature, you are a control freak; that means you like to control everything—

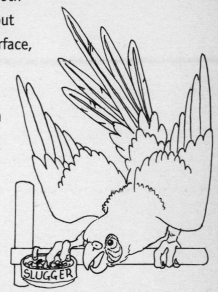

including your pets. However, your Aries pet, being true to its nature, refuses to be controlled—even by an omnipotent, invincible Scorpio. Have fun!

TAURUS: You and your pet will have a pleasant interaction. You're both very controlled, so you probably won't get in each other's way. And even though you will both enjoy each other's company, you're each secure enough to be alone when the circumstances call for it. Don't worry, though, Scorpio; nobody will—or can—steal your thunder; you'll still be the boss, even with a bull-headed, Taurean pet. 🦴 🦴 🦴

GEMINI: You'll tolerate your Gemini pet like a babysitter tolerates whoever she is babysitting.

You'll appreciate, up to a point, the playful demeanor of your pet dog or cat, until you have had enough. And when Scorpio's had enough, it's enough. Your Gemini pet won't give you much trouble as far as being disciplined. As much as they enjoy being frivolous and mischievous, they are also fast learners, particularly so with strong masters like yourself. This isn't the most evenly matched relationship between pet and owner. Still, all in all, you'll appreciate your Gemini pet for punctuating your days with moments of gaiety and lightheartedness. There aren't too many Scorpios who could wish for much more than that! 🦴 🦴

CANCER: You and your Cancer pet probably get along great. You'll provide the comfort and security that Cancers thrive on, and your Cancer animal companion will always (somehow) let you know how important you are to him or her. A good combo. 🦴 🦴 🦴

LEO: This could go somewhat better than if the tables were turned (you, Leo; pet, Scorpio). That's because human Scorpios usually have a rational side to them; animals don't rationalize anything, and even less so if they are Scorpionic. However, since you don't have to worry about that, you should fare relatively well with your Leo pet once you've set the ground rules and let him know that he (or she) absolutely can not be the boss! You'll have to break this animal in easily because Leo doesn't take well to having its power usurped. But being as noble and big-hearted as they are, your Leo the Lion dog, cat, bird or horse will eventually defer to you, all the while, never forgetting that he or she is just as tough as you are, without having to prove it. 🦴 🦴

VIRGO: As difficult as both you and your critter can be, you both get along remarkably well. You're both very persnickety: you, with everything, your animal, with food, where and how it sleeps, little annoyances from other pets (or humans). Even so, neither one of you seems to annoy the other; it's usually other factors that annoy you. So, you and your Virgo pet should do fine together. Although there's a mutual appreciation element to your relationship, you both keep out of each other's way, staying as close to each other as a "healthy distance" allows. Not a bad twosome. 🦴🦴

LIBRA: You would probably find a pet born under any air sign to be a bit too flighty or unstable. But of all three (Gemini, Libra, Aquarius), you'd do best with a Libra. Your Libra pet is not as serious as you, but his or her admiration and devotion to you will help keep your relationship afloat. Your Libra pet may be more vociferous than you'd like, but, then again, you're not all that easy to get along with, either. Even though you may get on each other's nerves from time to time, the love bond isn't likely to be broken. 🦴🦴

SCORPIO: Scorpio humans rarely get along well with other Scorpio humans. Now, a Scorpio human paired up with a Scorpio animal could be interesting.

Depending on how deeply entrenched in both your natures the Scorpio tenacity, aloofness and zeal are, you can determine how well you two get along. You can gage it yourself; you might even find it interesting, with Scorpio being a natural-born psychologist. If you find that your pet is every bit as overpowering and set as you are, and you want to stay friends with your pet, this may be a good time for you to learn to back down because chances are your pet won't. 🦴 or 🦴🦴

SAGITTARIUS: You and your centaur pet may have different energy patterns; you both have lots of energy, but it's directed in different ways. Even so, you two may experience a wonderful relationship, as long as you can keep up with your pet; he or she is sometimes all over the place, while you are set—

fixed—and aimed in one direction. One of you has to bend, and since the word "bend" doesn't even exist in Scorpio's vocabulary, it will always be your furry or feathered Sagittarian counterpart who will do all the bending. You just might have a hard time keeping him or her quiet most of the time. 🦴 🦴

CAPRICORN: Your Capricorn pet can come in one of two different packages: he or she is either very shy and retiring, or extremely determined and pushy. If it's of the first variety, you may not have much patience for it, and just let it do its own thing. If it's of the second variety, you'll have to gather all your Scorpio power to keep you on your toes with this one. You probably won't take to its coldness, no matter what the packaging of this animal; and it really couldn't care less that you are an all-powerful, all-knowing, indomitable Scorpion—with a stinger to boot! Your Capricorn pet will do just what it wants, when it wants, how it wants, where it wants, for as long as it wants—and no one takes longer than a Capricorn. I'd be leery of this one, Scorpio. ⊂⊐

AQUARIUS: An Aquarian pet is probably too scattered for your directed and very focused way of doing things. This animal won't center its attention on you, which is much to your chagrin. In fact, this animal won't focus on much of anything. You will either go crazy, totally ignore it, or, better yet, find a good Sagittarian, Gemini or Aries home for it. ⊂⊐

PISCES: You will love your Pisces pet almost as much as he or she loves you. This animal will always respond to your beckon call. Your Pisces cat, dog or even rabbit may so much as humble you, as Henry, the Pisces rabbit, so subtly humbled me. Your Pisces pet may even seem saintly to you. You will quickly forget your Scorpio prowess in the presence of these "heaven-sent" companions. Hold on to your Pisces pet, cherish it, recognize its superiority, and revel in the magic that exists between the two of you. ᏟᎮ ᏟᎮ ᏟᎮ

If I'm a SAGITTARIUS...

and My Pet Is:

ARIES: You two make a great pair! You both have lots of energy, you both love any kind of adventure (especially if it's outside), and you can both frolic together—ad nauseam. Even if you don't have a pet with whom you can chase rainbows (like a horse or a dog), you'll still feel a strong bond that connects you with your fiery friend; this is because you both have similar energies and modus operandi. You'll have a lot of fun with your Aries pet.

TAURUS: Your Taurus pet is probably too slow for your taste; he or she would rather take a nap than go fight giant windmills. You're too idealistic and often up in the clouds for this one. Your Taurus pet is very grounded, and doesn't even know what clouds are— even if your pet is a bird! You won't get a lot of enthusiasm from Taurus for most things, especially if they have to do with moving. The up side in this relationship is that you're flexible and forgiving, so you'll probably put up with your bull-headed pet, and love him or her just the same. 🦴 🦴

GEMINI: Here's a remarkably good combination. You and your Gemini pet will take to each other from moment you first meet. There is great chemistry here: your temperaments, energy levels and interests will jibe, and you'll always have

great times because you are both "playaholics."
Enjoy! 🦴 🦴 🦴

CANCER: As wonderful as these pets are, you,
Sagittarius, would probably do better with a pet
who is less demanding emotionally, as well as one
who is more energetic and fun. With your
sympathetic nature, however, you would welcome
any animal into your home and deal with it as well
as your malleable Sag ways would allow you to. The
exchange isn't the greatest here, but at least you'll
be friends. 🦴

LEO: You won't mind your Leo pet's sometimes
pompous, dogmatic attitude, so there should be no
problems between you. Just let your pet know (or
think) that he or she is King (or Queen), and your

little kingdom will remain in tact. If you do have another pet that could interact with this one, read up on their particular astrological sign so you'll know how (or how not) to pair them up with "Leo." With both you and your Leo pet being fire signs, there will be a constant high energy level, much excitement and enthusiasm between you. A good mix. ⬭ ⬭ ⬭

VIRGO: Don't expect your Virgo cat to want to play incessantly with you; don't expect your Virgo dog to necessarily want to run to the park with you every five minutes. *You* need to constantly be burning up lots of fiery, Sagittarian energy. Your Virgo pet just sticks its nose up in the air at the mere thought of rigorous exercise. Because of this, he or she is not your best counterpart. This pet is bound to be quite sedentary, enjoying the comforts of home, and an occasional walk around the block. This combination of energies may really make you want to climb a tree. ⌐⊐

LIBRA: Your energies are compatible, and so are your interests, to a certain extent. Your keyword is "action." Your Libra pet's keywords are "laziness," "comfort," and "a little bit of action." You can engage your pet in anything that you'd like to do, as long as it's not for an extended period of time. Neither one of you will demand much affection from the other; you're both relatively "cool" in that department. Not a bad match. ⌐⊐ ⌐⊐

SCORPIO: It will be a miracle if you two get together on anything. You are extremely flexible;

your Scorpio pet is extremely set. Your pet will try to always get its way, and will never defer to you; even though you are strong and often forceful, it is not in your Sagittarian nature to be domineering or controlling. You may or may not feel much affection toward your Scorpio pet since you don't necessarily find this one to be all that ingratiating. Maybe you should try another sign. ⌒

SAGITTARIUS: You'll have a jolly old time with your Sagittarian pet. If there is such a thing between animal and human, you'll feel as if you are soul mates. Even though there is somewhat of a difference in evolution here, you two will always be on the same wavelength. The two of you probably clicked the moment you met. You and your pet's relationship is based mostly on physical activity.

You love to run, hop, skip, jump and swim together. There's nothing amiss here. ⬭ ⬭ ⬭

CAPRICORN: For a Sagittarius, anything Capricorn can be a real drag. You need an animal that likes to move...a lot! Capricorns move, but not fast enough to suit you. Your Capricorn pet is not likely to be all that flexible, either. They're not real big on doing what others want them to do. They've got an incredibly strong mind-set; so, if they're aimed in a particular direction, nothing can sway them from their destination, whether that destination is the swimming pool, their food dish, the top of the hill, or even you! They really do like you; they just can't figure you out. This relationship could actually be quite comical—if you're on the outside looking in. ⬭

AQUARIUS: You and your Aquarian pet will be great together: no rules, no wet blankets, no limits...no peace. But who needs peace if you're a Sagittarian or an Aquarian? You two will make your own kind of "peace." You and your Aquarian monkey, pig, dog, cat or bird will harmonize like atonal music; it may sound odd to everyone else, but you'll feel perfectly comfortable making your own kind of "beautiful" music. Your Aquarian pet could end up being your best friend. 🦴 🦴 🦴

PISCES: You won't feel too free-spirited if you have a Pisces pet to take care of. You may feel more obligated than anything else. This pet would prefer to stay quiet and just "relax." The word "relax" doesn't even exist in your vocabulary. Your Pisces pet is also likely to be emotional and needy of your constant attention, something to which you could develop a strong aversion. You'll recognize the innate sweetness of this pet, but it's just too soggy for you. Try again.

If I'm a CAPRICORN...
and My Pet Is:

ARIES: If nothing else, you'll appreciate the boundless energy and spunk your Aries pet has. Capricorn values directness and strength. You both do well on your own; so, even though you may be "pals," you won't be missing each other while you're away all day doing what Capricorns do best: making money. Your Aries pet will be quite self-sufficient while he or she waits for you to come home and make dinner. You might not find your Aries pet at home when you get there, but he'll (or she'll) be back. This pet may roam, but it knows where its home is; he or she just likes coming and going as he or she chooses—just like you do! You're both on the cold, impersonal side, so neither of you will miss the closeness that other signs thrive on. Your relationship with your Aries pet seems to be more businesslike than anything else: friendly but cool. Good roommates. ⬭ ⬭

TAURUS: This is a really good pet for you, Capricorn. No matter what the species, you two will hit it off. Though your pet may be a bit more solicitous toward you than you toward it, you're both basically reserved and enjoy the quiet life. You don't have to worry about Spot running around the house like a maniac (like an Aries or Gemini). Your Taurus pet will enjoy certain luxuries, like stretching out on the couch or bed, or cuddling up with some cozy blankets and pillows. Try to let down your Capricornian stoicism and give in to your self-indulgent Taurean pet. If you allow him to live according to what is comfortable and natural for him, you'll have a much happier pet, and you, in turn, will be happier for it (and more popular with your pet, as well). 🦴 🦴 🦴

GEMINI: If you're a carefree kind of Capricorn—which really is a contradiction in terms—you *may* enjoy your frivolous Gemini pet. If you're not a carefree kind of Capricorn, a Gemini pet might be just what you need, anyway. This animal might actually make you smile, or even laugh; he or she may get you out of a rut by making you see that life really can be fun. Though you may not be suited temperamentally, there still might be something there between the two of you that will keep you friends—good friends. One thing that you both have in common is that neither of you emotes very much. Your Gemini pet is expressive, at least, but not all that affectionate. You're not even all that expressive; and when it comes to being affectionate, you'd rather be figuring out how much money you have in the bank. On the other hand, you may both rub each other the wrong way only *figuratively*. He's too active and expressive for you; you're too stodgy for your pet, never wanting to go for a walk or go out and play. A possible but not a probable match. 🦴 or 🦴🦴

CANCER: Cancer and Capricorn often match up well, whether the match is between humans, between animals, or between a combination of the two. Interestingly, you, Capricorn, are not all that emotional, but your Cancerian counterpart tends to be extremely so. Never could the saying "Opposites attract" be truer. You tend to be reserved and not all that responsive; your Cancer pet tends to be affectionate, wanting to cuddle and be near you as much as possible. Depending on your own particular psychological makeup, your sometimes whining, whimpering, needy, clingy pet will either annoy you or humble you, bringing you down from your lofty Capricornian perch. ⌬ ⌬ or ⌬ ⌬ ⌬

LEO: There may be a tug-o-war here regarding who's in charge. This invariably happens when both parties are under the influence of astrological signs that render them strong and domineering; the extent to which your animal behaves this way depends upon its species; therefore, some animals will be less of a problem than others. But even less developed animals like rabbits, tortoises or ferrets can—and do—express the Leo energy; it just won't conflict with a Capricorn human as much as if the animal were a dog, a cat or any other animal that has a stronger rapport with humans. As long as you discipline your Leo pet to understand that you are his (or her) boss, your ranking should be left intact. You should still allow this animal to think he or she is King (or Queen), as that is in keeping with your pet's Leo nature. Once the roles have been established, Leo will come around and show you unparalleled, unwavering devotion and loyalty. A strong bond could be established here. You both sense the other's strength and consequently a mutual respect is formed. ⊂⊃ ⊂⊃

VIRGO: Here's a good companion for you, Capricorn. Your Virgo pet knows you are the boss right from the outset. It is also very respectful of you and dutifully obeys your every command. Your cool temperaments match as well, and you both feel perfectly comfortable in each other's company. You'll both like to stay in for the most part; your Virgo pet isn't big on blazing trails— and neither are you, if you're a true Capricorn. This one's for you. ⬭ ⬭ ⬭

LIBRA: Your Libra pet could add some zip to your staid life as a Capricorn. You'll like this pet because he isn't hyper-kinetic, but he still is quite active and is bound to bring life and sparkle into your relationship. His (or her) gentle, sociable manner will melt that cool Capricorn heart of yours; and you'll like your Libran pet's affectionate nature: not too cold and not too mushy—just the right amount to add some flexibility to a stiff goat like yourself. This one will give you a lift. 🦴 🦴

SCORPIO: You're very similar to your Scorpio. You both like to dominate; you're both somewhat cold and aloof, though your feelings run deep; you're both kind of sneaky, and you both are set in your ways. Will you get along? Probably, since you both seem to relate to each other. You'll each end up doing whatever you choose; if your Scorpio wants to go on a walk—with or without you—he'll go. They're very good at doing things on their own; in fact, they prefer it that way. I wouldn't trust your Scorpio pet any farther than you could throw a horse; he knows he's not supposed to eat the cake that's been sitting on the kitchen table for a while; do you really think he's not going to go for it when your back's turned? Never underestimate a Scorpio—of any species. At any rate, you'll never cease to be either amused or baffled by your Scorpio pet.

SAGITTARIUS: Your Sagittarian pet may be too active and volatile for you to have a smoothly running relationship with him or her. Your stoic ways may not be too healthy for your pet, either, who simply wants to run around and play all day, instead of sitting around the house (which it could never do, anyway), watching you add up numbers on your computer. This pet should have an owner who is active, always on the go, and likes to take his or her pet along. If you have a Sagittarian pet that is not so inclined (such as a rabbit or a cat), you will still have your hands full, since this animal will be very active, sometimes to the point of being uncontrollable. You may be too much of a dyed-in-the-wool Capricorn to handle this bundle. Since it's virtually impossible for you to change your ways, consider getting an animal of a different sign. ⊂──⊐

CAPRICORN: You two Capricorns will feel comfortable with each other. If you have a Capricorn bird, he'll love to sit on your shoulder and help you figure out all those numbers. (Capricorns are extremely smart!) If it's a Capricorn dog that you've got, he or she will patiently and contentedly lie near you, at a safe Capricornian distance; you won't necessarily have to provide your pet with a bed; they're so stoic (just like you) that they'd rather lie on the hard, cold floor. If you've got a Capricorn cat, you may not even know she is around; these critters love to keep to themselves. Capricorn cats are perfect examples of the stereotypical ways in which cats are generally perceived to be: aloof, cold and unapproachable. You'll like your twin. ⌒⌒⌒

AQUARIUS: Here's an unlikely match if there ever was one. This animal may just push you over the edge. But you're so cool, you'd never jump. You'll just contain yourself, then put an ad in the paper for a nice Gemini, Sagittarius or Aries family to adopt a wacky, uncontrollable (at least by your standards) Aquarian pet. (Seriously, if you do ever find yourself in such a predicament, be sure to carefully screen any potential takers; the world's full of crazy people, who may not have the best intentions for your pet.) Capricorn, almost any pet would be more suited to you than an Aquarian. ⌒⊃

PISCES: Your Pisces pet will cool you down (if that's possible), warm you up, soften those hard Capricornian edges of yours, and generally just make you feel good all the time. This pet will be like a pair of comfy slippers. You'll be so fond of your Pisces pet that you couldn't imagine what life would be like without him or her. This is one pet you'd actually like to have near you all the time; he or she will want to be close to you, too, but won't whine or be demanding of you for much of anything. These animals are not the strongest of the bunch, so they usually just expect someone to take care of them. Your Pisces pet will be affectionate but not clinging. He or she will always allow you to call the shots, and will patiently wait for you while you're busy doing other things. A very special relationship.

If I'm an AQUARIUS...
and My Pet Is:

ARIES: You should have a great relationship with your Aries pet. You will both feed off of each other's exuberance and enjoy actively doing things together. You are quite flexible, so you shouldn't mind when your Aries pet gets antsy and wants you to play with him, take him to the park, or let him out of his cage for some rigorous hopping or wing-flapping. A good pair.

TAURUS: The one thing you and your Taurean pet have in common is that you were both born under "fixed" signs. This means that you are both set in your ways; that it is not necessarily good when neither of you will budge. But if push does come to shove, you will probably end up being the flexible one, since air (Aquarius) is always easier to manage than earth (Taurus). All that aside, you're bound to be much more active than your Taurean animal companion; so, there may be a lot of tugging, pushing, cajoling....and waiting on your part. You'll find that your Taurus pet is definitely wedded to the Earth. Plenty of frustration here.

GEMINI: Here's a fun one for you. You and your Gemini pet can frolic all you like, and you'll never tire of each other. Refer to the previous section on a Gemini owner with Aquarius pet.

CANCER: This match does not bode for the greatest success. You don't have the time nor the interest nor the emotional makeup to deal with a Cancer pet; they require a lot of time, tenderness and sensitivity, not that you don't possess these traits; they're just not at the top of your list. You're very active mentally; your Cancerian pet is likely to be very active emotionally. Neither one of you can truly relate to the proclivities of the other. Furthermore, your Cancer pet is not one for being ignored or left alone all day, something which you may have no problem doing. Lots of snags. 🦴

LEO: This can go well. Both you and your Leo pet have sparkling personalities, and so, you sparkle together. You'll love your Leo animal companion's vitality and abundant energy, and your pet will respond in kind to yours. He (or she) may want to rule the roost, but you'll go ahead and let him (or her) do it. You actually enjoy watching your pet prance, strut or march around the house, fully assuming the role of King (or Queen)! Even if you have a pet that wouldn't characteristically act that way, you'll still catch glimpses of certain Leo traits, like showing off or moving flamboyantly. Here's a case where master is more devoted to pet! 🦴🦴🦴

VIRGO: You love your Virgo pet, but you don't quite know what to do with it. It's so different from the way you are, or the way you'd expect it to be. Your pet is so calm, quiet...and sweet. You dream of having a pet who's a little boisterous, lively and not necessarily so sweet. You want to have fun; your Virgo pet wants to have dinner—quietly. A strange combination, to say the least. 🦴

LIBRA: You and your Libra pet are similar in a lot of ways. You are both more mental than physical, although, ironically, you both like to have fun frolicking in life's playground. Libra is more gentle and grounded than the remaining air sign, Gemini, so there won't be as much frenzy in your household as there would be with a Gemini pet around. (If you happen to also have a Gemini pet, the fun is tripled—and so is the clean-up.) Your Libra pet thrives on companionship, even though he or she is not known for being very tactile. Try to come up with just enough affection for your Libra pet to let him or her know how much you care. Although you prefer to do things on your own most of the time, this pet will suit you, and you may be the one seeking him out to spend some quality time together. 🦴 🦴 🦴

SCORPIO: If you were the Scorpio and your pet were the Aquarius, there would be reason for concern. With this combination, however, it may not be so bad. Even though your Scorpio pet may be very observant of your seemingly strange ways of doing things, this won't phase him or her. Your pet will just take your "Aquarianism" in stride and go along its business. There probably won't be much interaction between the two of you, but neither of you would probably want it any other way; you both need your space. Even so, you would like a pet that had a similar orientation as you, one who had more spunk and liveliness, rather than a vigilant, reclusive, enigmatic Scorpio. This will be strange. 🦴

SAGITTARIUS: You'll have a lot of fun with your Sagittarian pet. Your energies blend harmoniously and there is never any friction between you. This animal will be flexible enough to go along with any strange ideas your avant garde, Aquarian mind may come up with. Your pet is full of energy, and so are you. You may not have the physical stamina that your Sag pet has; but when you think the gallop around the track, the hike up the mountain or the boat ride is over, for your pet, the fun has just begun. No matter; you'll work it out. Good vibes here. 🦴 🦴 🦴

CAPRICORN: Aquarius, you might see your Capricorn pet as a wet blanket, especially if it's the kind of pet with whom you could see yourself sharing a lot of time. In the first place, your Capricornian pet won't be all that interested in sharing time—with anyone! He likes to keep to himself and stay secluded for the most part.

Although your Capricornian pet may go on ticking for a long time, his energy level is not all that high—at least not as high as yours. So, if you end up keeping this one, you'll be in one end of your house, and the pet in the other, unless he wants to eat, in which case this animal won't stop bugging you until it gets what it wants. Far from a match made in Heaven. ⊂==⊃

AQUARIUS: Two peas in a pod are you and your Aquarian pet. Only the two of you understand each other's quirks and idiosyncrasies. Only the two of you can watch neon lights together—for hours—and then, in a semi-frenzied state, run around the block ten times at two o'clock in the morning. If you don't have a pet that's quite up to those activities, you'll certainly find something else that will entertain both of you. You will find that even less active pets, like rabbits, will have a weird side to them if they were born under the sign of Aquarius. Being attracted to anything odd or eccentric, you may even have an odd animal, like a giraffe, a kangaroo or a porcupine. When both you and your pet are Aquarians, you may not even be all that "weird"; but there will be something different about both of you that will cause you to gravitate to each other. A strange attachment, but it works! 🦴 🦴 🦴

PISCES: You and your Pisces pet are probably like night and day. You run on nervous energy most of the day, and don't have the wherewithal to provide the constant, focused nurturing that your Pisces pet may require. Although your Pisces pet can do quite well on its own, it still needs you around—close by.

It needs to need you, and it needs to know that you care for him or her. You, for the most part, couldn't be bothered with all of that. You need an animal companion to share time with on a less intimate level. Your Pisces pet's calmness may drive you crazy. You crave much more stimulating company than that which a Pisces animal can provide. No way.

If I'm a PISCES...
and My Pet Is:

ARIES: Your Aries pet just might be too much for you to handle. He or she has a lot of energy, and always wants to do something with it—primarily of a rigorously physical nature. If you're true to your sign, you'll enjoy nature walks and strolls along the beach, but nothing that likens itself to your Aries pet's tastes. This animal would rather run, hop, fly, swim or slither until he or she literally has nothing left to go on—and that might take days! Unless your pet is small and easy to manage, you may find his or her need for constant activity quite draining. Try to hook up with a more low-keyed animal. ⊂∋

TAURUS: This will be a pleasing experience for you. Taureans, like you, prefer things more low-keyed than other signs (like Aries or Gemini). You thrive on peace and quiet, and your Taurus pet can probably fill that bill. You may not find him or her as flexible as you'd like; "stubborn" is the keyword for this animal. But with your adaptable and understanding ways, you'll probably give in to whatever stand this creature might take. Other than that, you and your Taurus pet's temperaments blend well; you both enjoy the easy life, and will probably enjoy spending the bulk of your time relaxing at home, or occasionally going on restful outings (if the type of animal permits). Your

Taurean pig, dog or bird will make few, if any, demands on you. He will tend to patiently wait...and wait...until you feed him, take him for a walk or pay any kind of attention to him. But, with you as his master, he won't have to wait long because you'll be there, doting on your precious Taurean pet, happily taking care of all his (or her) needs. A cushy relationship. 🦴 🦴 🦴

GEMINI: Although you'll constantly be amused by this animal's spunk, agility and intelligence, you may not have the wherewithal to go along with everything that its Gemini nature needs to express. Your Gemini pet is very active, both physically and mentally. It will always, eagerly and impatiently, be looking to you for something "fun" to do. Your Pisces nature is more in keeping with just lying low, and not being all that active—at least not as much as your Gemini pet. A run-of-the-mill relationship. ⌘

CANCER: Here's a match made in Heaven. You each provide what the other needs: companionship, affection and care. Your Cancer pet will love to cuddle up next to you, and will, in turn, welcome any affection from your end. There will be lots of cooing, purring, sighing, licking, pawing, nudging and nibbling. The atmosphere will always be one of peace and tranquillity. A perfect pair! ⌘ ⌘ ⌘

LEO: Your Leo pet may be too intense for your docile nature, though he or she will be ever protective of and devoted to you. You will pride yourself on having such a splendid creature. This animal has a high energy level, one which probably can't be matched by you; your Leo animal companion may meander about while you stay within the confines of your abode. At some point, though, the two of you will hook up again and relish each other's company. On many levels, this will be an enjoyable relationship. 🦴 🦴

VIRGO: There will be great chemistry between you and your Virgo pet, other than that the latter may be just a bit standoffish—something that you don't particularly take well to (at least when it comes to your pets). You'll both be inclined to spend quiet time together, puttering around the house and just "living a dog's life." You'll happily take good care of your Virgo pet, and your pet, in turn, will provide love and tenderness for you (unless it's one of those days when that picky Virgo influence will make him or her a bit aloof). You'll both enjoy trying out the same foods, lying out by the pool or in the grass, or snoozing on the couch together. A nice exchange of energies. 🦴 🦴 🦴

LIBRA: Your Libra pet enjoys the relationship factor in its life, but it won't feed into much of the affection or warm responsiveness that you might like from a pet. Being a very sociable animal, your Libra pet will want you to communicate with it...talk to it, sing to it; focus on it in a communicative way and your pet will be very happy. Just don't expect a whole lot in return when you want to cuddle or caress your pet. Air signs (like your pet) are not very tactile. Water signs (like you) are quite affectionate and tactile. You'll still spend quality time together, you'll enjoy being in each other's company and will always have a warm, lasting sense of companionship. A friendly exchange with few or no snags. ⊂⊐ ⊂⊐

SCORPIO: This doubling up will be comfortable as well as comforting. You and your Scorpio pet will blend like warm milk and honey. Your Pisces energy helps Scorpio let down its hair, fur or feathers, and makes a bowl of Jell-O out of what otherwise might be a bed of nails. Scorpio's intrinsic cold, detached manner (even in animals) comes undone with your soft, gentle, benevolent influence. Neither one of you is all that physically active, and you'll each welcome tender gestures of affection from your counterpart. This one will last. ⊂⊐ ⊂⊐ ⊂⊐

SAGITTARIUS: Your ideal image of the perfect pet is one who is gentle, calm, sensitive and responsive in an affectionate way. Your chances of finding such attributes in a Sagittarian pet are nil or close to none. This animal will definitely be responsive, but mostly in a physical, aggressive manner, devoid of any sense of "connecting" with you. Unless the animal is far above average, you won't get much in the way of tenderness or emotional feedback from a Sagittarian pet; such traits are paramount to most Piscean owners of any pet. This particular pet is too much "fire" for your watery nature. Success not likely here. 🦴

CAPRICORN: Your Capricorn pet's earthy nature blends well with your watery ways. Your pet will bask in your soothing company; you'll soften your pet's Capricornian tendencies, simply by being with the animal, by comforting and caring for it in an almost magical way that you Pisceans easily master. This pet may seem very obstinate at times; but, again, your deep insight, patience and understanding will work wonders on rounding out your pet's sharp edges. There's really not that much to work out between the two of you since the two energies of Capricorn and Pisces are naturally harmonious. If your Capricorn dog, cat, bird or whatever, pulls that goat-like stubbornness, the cool, still waters of Pisces (that's you) will soothe any trouble spots that this crusty, earthy critter may have. A potentially pleasing relationship. 🦴🦴

AQUARIUS: You may want to close yourself up in your house, and this time, leave your Aquarian pet either outside or in its cage! If you don't have a cage for it, you might consider getting one—no matter what kind of animal you have! Aquarius and you, Pisces, don't usually make for the greatest company; and if it's a "pal" you want, try looking elsewhere for a pet who's more compatible with you. Despite your patient, easy-going manner, an Aquarian pet might be the one who will prove that you're sainthood stops right there. This animal has a lot of kinetic energy that's not directed anywhere; the manner is dry, cool, distant...and often nuts. Your watery, warm, touchy-feely nature is definitely an enigma to your pet, and your Aquarian pet's "way" is a certain anomaly to you. Don't feel bad for giving up. ⌇⌐

PISCES: You'll either be too sappy for each other, or you'll both feed right into all the sappiness that your relationship with your Piscean pet will probably be based on. "Like attracts like." This saying couldn't be truer for you and your Piscean beast. It's not so much that you like each other. It's more like you *are* each other. Even though you're a human and your pet is an animal (but sometimes we wonder), you don't need anyone to tell you that the two of you are more like one. How that can be between human and animal is not only hard to understand, it's also very rare; but it does occur, and the likeliest case could be when both are under the astrological influence of Pisces. Pisces is a mystical sign; when you and your pet are both Pisces, you may sense that there is a "mystical" connection between you. At any rate, there will be an intense bond between you—one that you may even want to call "karmic."

Conclusion

THERE APPEARS TO be an intrinsic harmony that has always existed between animal and human; and no matter what the astrological combinations may be, we still regard our pets as a very special part of our lives. We may have a better rapport with some pets more than others, but the fundamental bonding is something that simply cannot be broken. The unconditional love, trust and devotion that our pets unequivocally express to us compels us to respond in kind. If only we could be this humble and practice it with our fellow human beings. It seems we must look to our "lower" forms of life on this planet in order to raise ourselves to a higher level of consciousness.